One Sheaf, One Vine

Racially Conscious White Americans Talk About Race

Robert S. Griffin

ISBN: 1-4107-4419-1 (Paperback)

This book is printed on acid free paper.

1stBooks – rev. 12/15/03

Let the corn be all one sheaf—
and the grapes be all one vine,
Ere our children's teeth are set on edge
By bitter bread and wine.

From *The Stranger* by Rudyard Kipling

To Denis Ruiz

CONTENTS

1   INTRODUCTION

This book is made up of personal statements about race from seventeen racially conscious white Americans. By racially conscious I mean that, for them, the fact that they are white—other terms, European American, Euro—is more than an incidental, insignificant, or peripheral aspect of their being. Their racial identity is central to how they view themselves and conduct their lives. The people you will meet come from virtually every part of the country. None of them knew any of the others when this project began (I introduced several to one or two of the others after I had gathered the material for the book).

What you will read is drawn from an audiotape-recorded conversation I had with each of these individuals separately (in one case it was a couple). Conversation is a more accurate term than interview for what went on between them and me. I didn't have an interview protocol that I used with everyone. There was nothing so formal as that. Instead, I was guided by a list of topics and themes I wanted to explore with each person. I edited myself out of the transcription of each tape so that it was just a statement, or personal account, from the person I talked with. I gave each statement a title and wrote a brief preface to introduce the speaker. After transcribing nine of the tapes myself, I suddenly lost virtually all my hearing and could no longer hear the voices on the tapes. I am appreciative of Katrina Gibson's excellent work transcribing the last seven tapes, as well as for her editorial assistance.

The words in this book are the speakers'. I did some editing for length and to avoid repetition and maintain continuity, but I was careful not to alter, soften, or censor anything someone said. As much as possible, I want you to experience these individuals as I did, and reading back over the statements, I think you will.

This book grows out of another book I authored, *The Fame of a Dead Man's Deeds: An Up-Close Portrait of White Nationalist William Pierce*, which was published in 2000. William Pierce, who died in July of 2002, was a prominent figure in the white nationalist (another term, white racialist) movement. He was the founder and chairman of the National Alliance, which has around two thousand members and is headquartered on Pierce's 340-acre property in rural West Virginia. Pierce is best known as the author of the widely read—a half million readers—underground novel, *The Turner Diaries*, which describes the racially motivated terrorist acts of a band of white American revolutionaries against a corrupt federal government and its supporters.

In the process of researching the Pierce book in the late 1990s, I met a number of white racialists, some followers of Pierce and some not. After the book was published, other racially aware whites contacted me, and I met still others at various meetings and through the Internet. What has struck me about the three hundred or more people I have encountered over the past five years, and I include the leaders of the movement in this characterization, is how invisible and silent they are in the public arena. To be sure, we have a generalized image of people of this sort and what they believe: ignorant, violence-prone KKK members, menacing skinheads, and low-life or deranged thugs doing their "perp walks" after committing a heinous hate crime against minorities. The vast majority of the white nationalists I have met do not fit these stereotypes, but how would average Americans know that? These people aren't on the television news shows speaking for themselves. They don't make movies. They don't publish books and articles. Politicians don't articulate their perspective and advocate their positions. Journalists and intellectuals don't write about them unless it is to belittle them. They aren't on university and college faculties, and schools make no attempt to consider them objectively.

What has also struck me about the people I have met is that, at least in my view, they have something to say that would contribute to the public dialogue and debate. I believe this society and culture would benefit from hearing what they think about race. Which is not to say that I consider them to be right about everything. I do offer, however, that, in the main, white racialists are serious and thoughtful and sincere, and they are trying to live just and honorable lives. If

2

you find this to be true of the people in this book, know that they aren't exceptional. They are typical.

Denis Ruiz, whom I met in late 2000, sparked the idea of writing this book. Denis, a rather shy and reserved computer programmer from the Philadelphia area, had read the Pierce book in its original e-book format and offered to help me clean up its many typos and misprints for the print version of the book that was published in 2001. After the editing task was completed, Denis and I stayed in contact, communicating just about every day by phone or e-mail. I found him to be a remarkably bright and reflective and decent human being. Denis became a highly valued colleague and friend. He gave me direction and support in both my professional and personal life.

In the spring of 2002, I decided that I wanted others to know the person I had come to know. I would write a book that introduced Denis and some of the other racially aware white people I had met or would seek out. I didn't want this book to be about leaders of the white nationalist movement such as Pierce but rather everyday people like Dennis. Mainstream America wasn't hearing from them and I thought that it should have that chance. Denis was my first interview, or conversation, and I took it from there. I started contacting people and asking them whether they would be interested in being in the book (not one person said no) and if they knew of anyone they could recommend to me. The monthly newsletter *American Renaissance* generously put a full-page notice in one of its issues that I was seeking people. The word spread that I was writing this book. Every day for months I received inquiries from people who wanted to be interviewed.

In selecting those to include, I looked for people of various ages and walks of life and regions of the country, and both men and women. Some of them have asked me not to use their real names because they are worried about retaliation for expressing their beliefs, that they might lose their jobs or their children might be harassed. If they left it up to me to use their real name or not, in every case I chose not to. I didn't want anyone to pay a price for supporting my work and doing what I think is the right and responsibility of us all: to speak out on the issues of the day. I have placed an asterisk next to a name the first time it is mentioned if it is a pseudonym.

As much as anything, this book is about what is allowed into the public discourse in America and what is excluded from it. In that light, the publishing history of both the Pierce book and this one bears recounting. My literary agent was enthused about the merits and commercial prospects of the Pierce book. However, fifteen major publishing houses he submitted the manuscript to all passed on it saying that while the book was a meritorious effort there simply was no market for it. Nobody would be interested in buying it, they told him. I suspected that the real reason for the turndowns had much more to do with the content of the book than with its sales potential. The real problem with the manuscript, I speculated, was the unfiltered reports of Pierce's criticisms of blacks and, especially, the Jewish influence on American culture and foreign policy, which made it very unpalatable to editors and publishing houses.

I think publishers should be free to publish whatever they want for whatever reason they choose. At the same time, I believe that no individuals and groups, whether it's blacks or Jews or anyone else, should be free of critique and criticism. Critique and criticism are crucially necessary to a free and democratic society. I also believe the American public needs to be aware that certain topics and arguments are not reflected in the mainstream media. That is crucially important because so much of what we know, or think we know, is not derived from our direct experience but from mediated contact with reality. We haven't seen or heard it ourselves. Someone has shown it to us and told us about it, whether in a book or an article, or on television or in a movie, or in a classroom.

Whatever the real reason for the publisher turndowns of the Pierce book, I was left with a manuscript that I thought was worthy of being made available to the reading public. There had been an earlier manuscript of mine, about education, that hadn't gotten published and that I believed had been blocked because of its ideas rather than its quality, and I wasn't going to let that happen again if I could help it. A colleague told me about an Internet company that, for no charge, made manuscripts available through its web site in electronic book— e-book—format. So very late one evening, alone in my office at the university, I followed the instructions on this company's web site and submitted a computer file of the Pierce manuscript. And as it turned out, despite all the dire predictions from editors, the Pierce book has sold extremely well in both e-book and print form.

I decided to make another run at commercial publishers with this Sheaf book, as I eventually came to call it. I clung to the hope that I could get the imprimatur of a major New York publishing house, a spot on the shelves of Borders or Barnes & Noble, and perhaps even a review in *The New York Times*. So I wrote up a "pitch" letter for my agent to send along with sample sections from the book to editors to try to induce their interest. After reading what I had put together, my agent begged off from representing the manuscript. He said that the concept and samples were very good indeed, but that this manuscript would be "a very tough sell."

I contacted a few publishing houses on my own and they responded that this was excellent material, but they couldn't risk publishing anything like this. They said that whether or not the people in the book are in fact racists and anti-Semites, they would certainly be accused of being just that, and the publishing company would be attacked for getting behind this material, and they didn't want to go through that hassle. And besides, there undoubtedly would be major problems with distribution, as bookstore chains would be pressured not to put it on their shelves.

I had been through this racist and anti-Semite business with the Pierce book, so I was somewhat prepared for it. Both of those epithets, as well as the rest of the litany—hater, bigot, Nazi, extremist—were relentlessly applied to Pierce. And since I was the author of a book about him and thereby associated with him, I got a taste of name-calling attacks myself in articles and interviews and when I was the subject of radio talk shows. I have come to the conclusion that these slurs are used to demonize, marginalize, and intimidate people and set them up for punishment. In my case, these smears put the focus on me, whether I had impure thoughts and what ought to be done with me, and distracted attention from the substance of what I was writing and the legitimacy of the motives and tactics of the people who were attacking me. By the time I had finished the Sheaf book, I wasn't about to run scared or kowtow to anyone who tried to silence me or the people I write about. If this country stands for anything it is freedom of conscience and the open discussion of ideas. And if this country demands anything from each of us it is to do what we do what we think is right, and I think publishing this book is the right thing to do.

So I have self-published this Sheaf book through an Internet publisher as I did the Pierce book. It gives you the chance to determine for yourself whether the people in this book have anything worthwhile to say, and whether what they say has any implications for what you believe and the way you live your life.

2   DISPLACED

Denis Ruiz is a fifty-year-old computer programmer who lives with his wife and teenage daughter near Philadelphia. A short time before this interview, he learned that he has non-Hodgkins lymphoma, a form of cancer. He was in significant pain at the start of the interview, and I wasn't sure that he could complete it. But as the interview progressed his voice became stronger and stronger, and his manner became that of someone completely well.

I grew up in the 1950s in a little town called Fairview Village in south Jersey. It is separated from the south end of Camden by a creek that borders the town on the north, west, and south. There used to be a shipyard at the south end of Camden, and when the United States entered World War I in 1917 and '18, there was the sense that there was a need to be building more ships there. The area south of Camden was pretty rural at that time, so they built a development there. It was a planned community, designed by a fellow named Litchfield. It was a very beautiful little town. The idea was that if people were going to work in the shipyard, they ought to have a nice environment in which to live. It had what I guess you could call garden community-type architecture. The houses were all made of brick and attached to one another in clusters of four, and sometimes two, like twins. So the houses were in rows, but they were broken up. They all had yards, and there were commons areas on every block where they didn't build houses, and some blocks didn't have houses at all. There was just grass and trees in those places.

People would walk their dogs there and kids would play touch football or tackle. They planted all these oak trees, lovely trees, so by the time I lived there they were mature, maybe sixteen to eighteen inches in diameter. There was a town square with park benches, and people would go there and sit and talk and get to know one another, and there were stores and businesses—it was a socially and economically self-contained little unit. Looking back on it, the neighborhood where I grew up seems idyllic with its parks and shaded streets in the summer and all. In fact, one fellow who had lived in England remarked that Fairview Village was like a little English town.

My parents bought their house there after World War II. They were typical of the kind of people who lived in the neighborhood when I was growing up: second and third generation immigrants from Europe. All of my grandparents came to America around the turn of the century. My mother's parents were from Slovakia and my father's parents were from Spain by way of Cuba. There were no opportunities for typesetters in Cuba, so my grandfather went to Philadelphia. We were a minority in the neighborhood, as most people were Italian, Polish, or Irish, and there were a few Scottish people. But we fit in because, like the others, we were recently arrived Europeans. All of us who lived there saw ourselves as Americans. That was the glue that kept us all in it together, that and the fact that everybody spoke English. Nobody put any emphasis on other languages.

Although my neighborhood was all white, I grew up, as much as I can tell, without prejudice against people of other races. We had what could be called a European code of conduct. At the core of this code is that you evaluate people one at a time. You judge someone on his own merits, not as part of some group. I remember one time my parents called a TV repairman and the guy who came was black. My parents were fine with that. The set got fixed. That was what mattered to them.

My grandparents and parents were working class people, but they never had any trouble finding work because they were in a trade that was in demand, even during the depression years. There was a big value in my family on trade unionism, which made us side with the Democrats, who were associated with trade unionism. The Republicans seemed anti-union, advocating open shops and things like that. Closed shops—forcing people working someplace to be in a union—didn't seem to us like a bad thing to do because we saw open shops as a way to undermine unions. So we could get behind a kind of hardball liberalism as being morally justifiable. Even though my family basically sided with the liberals, it wasn't all the way. There was some conservatism there at the same time. My uncle on my mother's side didn't belong to a union. He was a free agent who worked for various places on terms he worked out. My parents thought that was good, too.

My family was always looking to be fair. That was really important to us. In the 1950s and early '60s, that came into play because it was the time of civil rights and fairness was the big theme in all that. I see now that besides fairness there were issues around race and culture: could, and should, such different people mix together in society? But being in a new terrain in this country, my people didn't have a taste for the full flavor of the history of America and didn't know that there were reasons why the races had been segregated up to that time. Everything was couched in terms of fairness back then. That is how the issue was framed on television and everywhere, and my parents bought into that way of looking at it. And from that angle, the civil rights issue was like if a person wants to paint your property and he has the proper tools and references from other jobs he has done, and there are bids and you pick the one who is clearly better and he comes in and he's black, should you not go ahead and hire him and have him do the job? We got the sense that in the past this black guy would automatically be ruled out as soon as it was apparent he was black. That violated our sense of the proper way to live. You should judge a person on his own merits. If somebody has a sledgehammer and is breaking the rocks and getting the work done, you respect that. To do anything else isn't proper, it isn't fair.

Plus, my parents were big supporters of John Kennedy. They thought he was going to be a salvation. He was young and forward-looking, and he was Catholic, that played some role in it. We were Catholic, and here for the first time was a Catholic president. Kennedy seemed to be on the side of the civil rights movement, and so that had an effect on us.

And something else that got us on the side of civil rights was what I now see as a white or European trait—at least in the second and third generation sort that made up my neighborhood—and that is to be disposed to think we should all kick in and do the right thing and make something work. Also, we had the tendency to placate and smooth things over and keep the peace and keep things moving along and not get in the way.

Our impulse all along had been to bury our heritage and minimize our differences with others and become full-fledged Americans. That orientation went along with the racial message we were getting from the media and liberal politicians and the churches that racial differences don't matter. They are just a different paint job; it is the same car. I think we would have been less receptive to the big agenda that we were going to live among blacks and everything was going to be peachy keen if we had lived in America for two hundred years and knew the score better than we did.

Although as I think back on it, we knew that when a neighborhood gets mixed, it is bad news. My grandparents had seen what happened where they lived in Philadelphia—they went there in the '20s—when the area became flooded with black people from the South. Their children moved out of the area because it had been taken over by blacks and they knew that neighborhood wasn't for them any more. My mother grew up in Camden in a largely Polish neighborhood. Puerto Ricans moved in and the whole place went to shit.

In the late 1950s, economic changes had a big effect on my hometown. The shipyard folded, as did another place where a lot of people worked, an iron and forge plant. So the town was weakened. But I think it would have eventually rebounded by the end of the 1970s when other kinds of businesses reflecting the changes away from industrialization would have come into that area. Like the business I am in, the computer business. But that never happened because a second process was at work: the integration of non-whites into the town.

Before it became illegal, local realtors would show houses only to white families. Although it has been painted as an unfair arrangement, it really reflected the point of view of the people who lived in the town. The people there wanted to live among their own people. They wanted to live in a white community. Now, I see that as the highest form of self-determination: people defining their own community, people deciding what comes into their collective lives, people determining their own standards. It doesn't matter if their standards are rational or moral by someone else's measure. People have a right to decide whom they are comfortable living next to and not comfortable living next to. This is fundamental and it is not a matter of rationality or of morality. It is simply human. It's not that they have ill will toward anyone. It is just that they know what atmosphere they like. They might, for instance, prefer to live among Catholics or with people who are compatible with some other of the churches in a town.

When realtors were screening people and only showing houses to whites, it wasn't the dark conspiracy it has been painted as being. Rather, it was a matter of realtors being true to the community, being part of the community. But of course the issue never got defined in those terms, and in the late '60s-early '70s there were lawsuits, and realtors had to sell houses to blacks and anyone else who was interested in moving in there. A lot of the blacks that have moved in there have been "section eights." Section eight is part of a law where the government encourages integration by paying the rent of minorities who move into white areas. That has turned out to be a deadly poison administered to the Fairview Village of my youth.

The neighborhood where I grew up has turned into a wasteland. Whites still make up a majority of the community—55%—but nevertheless the neighborhood has gone in the same direction of a typical urban black area. When I was living there, when a tree died an Irish guy named Fred Fagan would plant a new one. Now, those saplings are mighty trees. When a tree dies these days, no one plants a new one. There is broken glass all over the place, and things like busted up shopping carts lying on their side blocking the alleys. Many of the old brick houses are covered over with some kind of god-awful siding. When I was a kid, repairs and restorations were done in the mode of the existing architecture of the town. Now, from one house to the next, they are all different. There is no common thread to the look of the houses now. There used to be hedges and white picket fences that lent a common feel to the area—no more.

My mother still lives there, and when I go back to visit her, I have the feeling when I get out of my car, "Is this an ambush? Is someone going to jump me?" Recently, a black teenager knocked my mother to the ground, injuring her, and took her purse. This sort of thing was unheard of in the old neighborhood, but it is commonplace now. My mother never had to contend with that kind of thing before. The black woman across the street was just arrested for robbing 7-Eleven stores with an accomplice. When I was growing up, kids could go anywhere in town on their bicycles. We could go in the woods and explore down by the creek and there would be no danger at all. Now, there is no way you would allow your child to even take a walk around the neighborhood. Just this year, a young white woman was abducted by two black men and taken to the place where we used to play ball and raped and murdered. These heinous crimes are happening regularly there. Who are these people?

There is no sense of connectedness among the people in my old hometown. There is this white teenager just down the street who not long ago hung himself in his bedroom. The word is he spent a lot of time alone listening to rap music. So much of popular music these years is dark and sinister and negative, with fragmentary images that confuse and bamboozle, and for someone already on the edge, like I assume this kid was, that can be deadly. In the old days, the risk of a terrible thing like that happening would have been much less. A boy like this wouldn't have been without the context of a supportive white community and way of life.

Back in 1967 or so, I listened to Jim Morrison—he was the lead singer of The Doors—and took what he sang very seriously, as if it were a volume of Keats or Walt Whitman. In those years, white groups were covering a lot of black music. I remember this one Morrison song. I think the name of it was "Alabama" or something like that. The message of the song was "I must have whiskey and your wife." The lyric was rock bottom, about drunks going from house to house looking for alcohol and sex, and there is Morrison recasting it in a way that glamorizes and legitimizes scum of the earth. That was what I was taking in. But I lived in a place that counteracted that poison. I had something the boy down the street didn't have. But the place I had has been destroyed, obliterated.

There is no good reason why I shouldn't have been able to do what my mother dreamed I would do: come back and live near her in the town where I was born. There is no good reason that I shouldn't have been able to buy a home and raise my child in the same town I grew up in. There is no good reason that Fairview Village, New

Jersey shouldn't have continued pretty much on the track that it had been on for forty years up to the 1960s and '70s. There are no good reasons for any of that, but there are bad reasons, bad reasons I have come to understand in the last few years.

Back in the 1960s, when I was a teenager, and on into the 1970s, I picked up the strong sense that there was a major revolution going on in this country. A change was in the air. There was going to be a reorientation in the society. There was a turntable that was rotating and was going to keep on rotating. A lot of self-assured media figures were telling me that. I especially remember ranting types like Jerry Rubin and Abby Hoffman and Malcolm X. There was a lot of revolution talk, and I decided this must be what was going on.

Looking back on it, I can see that what they were talking about wasn't what was going on at all. It was like the Wizard of Oz, a big presentation being put on to give the illusion that some big thing was happening. What was really going on was a lot of people who had access to a microphone telling me what was going on. In those years, I didn't understand what media was and how they shaped reality for people. Media for me was like water for a fish in a tank. I didn't comprehend that someone was adding color to it and creating illusions so I swam around in a certain way.

When Jimmy Carter got into office, I thought he was a good guy because he seemed like a moral man. I suppose to some extent that perception came out of my Christian upbringing, the idea of living a morally upright life. That helped keep me in the liberal camp. Although, by that time I was living on my own and the contradictions between reality and what I was being told were increasingly apparent.

Lyndon Johnson's talk back in the '60s about the Great Society had registered deeply with my dad. To him, it was a kind of trade unionism for the country, the idea that there would be health care for the aged and so on. But it started to hit me that there was something wrong here. I thought to myself, all this stuff costs enormous amounts of money, and all these programs that were going to fix poverty and the black problem and all the rest aren't working. Not only are the ghettos still here, they are worse than ever. There is a flaw in the liberal agenda somewhere. And then Reagan came along saying that all these programs were just making things worse, and that confirmed what I had been thinking.

Any level of white racial consciousness wasn't there yet for me—I'm talking about in the 1980s. Coming out of my childhood, I had an awareness that there were Italians and Irish and Polish, but I had no real sense of being white. As for blacks, I just saw them as different. They had a different accent and cooked different food and went to a different church and conducted themselves differently. I really didn't go any farther than that in those years. But I did think about the fact that trying to improve their situation along the lines of LBJ's vision seemed to be making things worse for them. Here we were, twenty years later, and the nuclear family with a present and working father that had once been the norm among blacks was falling apart. Standards with reference to blacks seemed to be lower than before. Conduct that at one time would have been simply condemned came to be attributed to circumstances beyond blacks' control, whether it was white racism or something else.

I like classical music and in the 1980s I listened to public radio because it was the last stronghold for classical music. I had the button on my car radio set to the public station. But then a strange thing happened: public radio all but abandoned classical music. They dropped it for all voice, which, as I look back on it now, was all liberal propaganda. An endless number of shows came on out of nowhere. There were Terri Gross's interviews, and there was a woman named Mary Moss Kahane, and I remember a family therapist named Dan Gottlieb. I didn't simply tune out the station because public radio had put itself across as reflecting an enlightened point of view, so I got the idea that if I wanted something more in depth and thoughtful than the snippets I could get on the other stations, I should listen to public radio. So these people had my ear.

What I find interesting now is that it was not that I really chose to listen to these people. It was more that they just sort of sprung up. It is sort of scary to think about how it happened. It is like the legend where the guy throws dragon teeth and everywhere the dragon teeth land a warrior springs up. It is as if someone threw some dragon teeth and these radio personalities sprung up where I had been innocently listening to classical music. I was getting a heavy dose of their point of view and I didn't know where it was coming from or why.

White racial consciousness didn't happen for me until 1997, I think it was. There is a guy I work with whom I really respect—very bright and capable and accomplished, a ham radio operator, a wonderful, likable soul with a great manner. One day, I followed a link on his bookmarks page on his computer and went to a web site called the White Nationalist Library. The site contained a bunch of essays on white nationalism. I started reading them and it was clarity and sunshine. Here was somebody explaining the history of the last few decades accurately and in a way that I could understand. I felt like a fool. I was kicking myself that I hadn't figured all this out on my own.

That started it for me, and in the years since then I have been reading and thinking and talking to people and looking at things in a new way, and race has become a lens through which I look at the world and my own life. I have concluded that a war is being waged against whites in America, against European Americans. It is not being conducted violently, and it is being conducted at a very slow speed. But it is a war nevertheless. In a war, there is demographic turmoil: populations get displaced, people flee. The neighborhood that was destroyed in my hometown and the refugees that were created are a component of that war. Exactly who is waging this war against whites, I really don't know. But I do believe that blacks, and more recently Hispanics, are being used as weapons against the racial and cultural world created by European people on this continent, and against the white people who live here now. A sophisticated Marxist–type struggle is going on against white people, but instead of class warfare it uses ideas as weapons—racism, oppression, multiculturalism, diversity, white privilege, and so on. It manipulates, even creates, ethnic and racial grievances against whites and uses them to bludgeon white people.

What had been submerged all of my life—my race and my heritage—has become front and center. Before, I was just an American. Now, I am a *European* American. Before I was just a man. Now I am a *white* man. I admit I have cringed and retreated some in my time, but that was mostly because I couldn't figure out what was going on. Now I realize that I am part of a people who are being attacked and that truly they are my people, and I stand and draw the line.

The place I live in now, on the outskirts of Philadelphia, was a clean and safe place when my wife and I moved here fifteen years ago. But the pattern of my childhood home has been repeated. Non-whites have moved in and the neighborhood has deteriorated drastically. Before, there were a fair number of lower-end, poor white people, but they were never a problem. But we have problems now.

More and more, I find that this isn't a suitable place for my family. It doesn't reflect our heritage and values. The Catholic school here pushes multiracialism and doesn't put emphasis on academic excellence. My daughter went there for a time. She reported to her mother and me that the black boys were aggressive and that she didn't like them. That certainly didn't come from us. We hadn't said a word to her about race.

We learned first hand, and the hard way, that these liberal, multicultural schools don't work. We realized that we wanted a school of our own flavor. Unfortunately, the school that provides the closest thing to a European-type education is thirty-five miles away from where we live. So every day either my wife or I drive that thirty-five miles there and back. When we moved to this house, it was a nine-mile drive for me to work. Now, with the big expansion of office parks, it is twenty miles.

There is no neighborhood here at all for me now. A neighborhood is where your friends are and where your kid goes to school and where you work—that's what makes a neighborhood. My line of people needs to be bound to the earth. I need to belong to a certain soil, to a certain region, to a locality, and I need to stay in that locality, and for that process to go on for generations. I really believe that that my desire to be literally grounded is a basic white or European impulse, and that it has been irradiated in my people to a great extent over the last three decades or so. Part of this is due to economic factors, the globalization of the economy, and there are cultural factors, increased consumerism and individualism; and, in ways I don't fully comprehend, I sense these phenomena are part of this war against whites I have been talking about. In any case, I have to go to some other part of the country to find work. Really, I am migrant worker.

What a lot of whites have been doing is building gigantic houses on three-quarter acre lots in the far reaches of the suburbs. My take on that practice is that, whether these people fully realize it or not, doing that makes them pretty much impervious to encroachment; blacks are not going to come there. But these white people lose in the process too, because they have to own a $350,000 house to pull this off and they wind up house-poor, with no money left after they pay the mortgage each month. All that money going into the house could be going into having a richer life on another level. If they could live in an old style house, they could get by on one salary with no trouble. They wouldn't have to work two jobs. If they could build a simple three bedroom semi-detached house in a town like the one I grew up in, where the lots are small and there are little gardens and walkways and so on, they could have something that is affordable, plus they could experience something really worthwhile: living in a tight knit community of white people.

My wife and I know that if we move we won't get more than we paid for our house fifteen years ago because of what has happened to the neighborhood. If it hadn't been for the literal destruction of my world, I would have been in much better financial shape that I am in now. My mother's house, when she dies, would have sold for a pretty penny, but it is worth very little on the market now. And if we move, I don't want to end up in a situation like my mother is in now in my childhood home, and like I am in, where the neighborhood is declining and I have to either stay and feel trapped or get out. I'd like to grow apple trees, and it takes years to do that, and you can't take your trees with you when you move. So we are probably going to rent the best place we can find near where I work and also buy a rural place and go there on the weekends and fix it up, and then move there permanently when I retire in fifteen years.

I'd like a house in a place that is like turning the clock back fifty years. I have been going to homestead sites online and reading homesteading magazines to get guidance and inspiration as well as to get some mental distance from the situation I'm in now. I'm reading about people who are forming small communities in places like

Kentucky. I subscribe to mailing lists for homesteading and homesteaders, and I correspond with people who are actually doing this to get a sense of what homesteading entails and what their lives are like. They are all white, and while they don't talk about race, I speculate that at least to some extent there is a racial impulse giving impetus to what they are doing. Some homesteaders in rural Pennsylvania have invited me to visit, which I plan to do when I get through my current health issue.

It saddens me to think that I can no longer live in the place where my mother lives and where I grew up. There would be nothing more rewarding to me than to have a property like that passed down to me in the condition that it was once in. With each of the places my family has lived in, we have made material improvements, such as putting in a nice garden or gutting the walls and putting in new sheet rock and improving the drainage. Over decades, these changes add up to significant improvements: a better garden, a vineyard, fruit trees, a nice deck. By staying in one place, your property improves and you improve the community, and you form deep, lasting connections with people. That is the basic way our ancestors in Europe lived for centuries. They were tied to a place. There was a real value in that. Now, we sell places and move, at best to buy a better place. But personally I feel that I am all the time planting and I am never going to get the harvest and I am never going to live in a true community.

I talked with my daughter about the rural place I'm thinking about buying or building. I said to her, "If mom and I get a place like that, would you like to stay there, live there after we are gone?" She said, yes, she would. She was receptive to that idea and she is only seventeen years old. I think she understands what has happened to us, where we have had to pick up and start over, and she doesn't want to get in that same pattern. That house will be twenty years of our labor, where we plant nice gardens and fruit trees and a vineyard, and make structural improvements. And while we are doing that, we will be in a community where we are with people who see the world as we do, and we will know people and they will know us. And then we will give the house to our daughter. I'll bet when my wife and I pass she won't just sell it and move on. She will consider it the place where she should live and she'll build on it herself. My sickness has come out of nowhere, but once I get over this, I'm going to get that house.

Denis didn't get the house. He died a couple of months after telling me this.

3   I WANT TO ASK, "WHY?"

Laura Hayes* is thirty-four years old and lives with her husband near Tampa, Florida. They have no children. Laura is about to complete a graduate program in business administration and works part-time as a sales clerk.

I was raised in northern Indiana and had contact with very few minorities growing up. There were some blacks that had spilled over from the Chicago area living there, but they tended to stay in a separate area of town. I would see them shopping, but that was about it. There were a few Asians who I believe worked at a nearby science laboratory, but I didn't have any contact with them either. That area is now heavily settled with Hispanics, but there were none there when I was growing up.

There were no minority children in the elementary, middle, or secondary parochial schools I attended. A few black people went to the church I attended, but they had the same decorum as the others in the church, and so I really didn't give it a thought. As for interracial dating, there was an understanding that they are who they are and we are who we are and interracial dating or sex just isn't appropriate. But that was all unstated. Nobody ever told me that. It just wasn't part of my thinking growing up to have dated out of my color.

Really, race wasn't a concern when I was young. Remember, this was a couple of decades ago, and all the government agendas weren't being rammed down our throats as they are now—multiculturalism, intolerance, diversity, immigration, and so on—or at least they weren't where I was in Indiana. As for the media promoting any kind of racial agenda, I suppose it was there, but I don't remember it registering with me at that time. Thinking back on it, I didn't have what could be called a racial identity in those years. Nearly all of the people I was around were white. I was white. I didn't think about it. That is just the way it was.

When I was young, life just kind of rolled along. We were all marching to the same drummer, I guess you could say. We shared a definition of the world. We were all clean and orderly and law-abiding. We all dressed nearly the same. We were friendly to one another. We went to one another's houses. We felt safe and secure. Doors were left open. I never worried about violence or shootings at school. I knew that, in years past, in the 1960s and '70s, the public high schools in town had suffered racial tension, but I was sheltered from that kind of thing during my years in school. I didn't have to ponder what was going on in society, think, "Oh, I see a trend here," anything like that. I was typical of the kids I grew up with. We just lived our lives.

College for me was also in northern Indiana. There were some blacks there and I did have a sense of their difference, their "otherness." They spoke differently and had a different way about them. But again, I didn't really think about it. It just was. After I left college, I moved to southern California and lived there for four years. That area was much more of a melting pot than I had been in. I was brought into contact with many different types of people. But people pretty much stayed in their own group. There was no rioting or anything like that when I was in California—this was after the Rodney King violence. I was in my mid-twenties at that time. No racial light had come on up to that point.

While I was in California, a friend of mine invited me to go with her to some Bo Gritz seminars. His focus was on government conspiracies and cover-ups and self-sufficiency and survival. He didn't have a racial agenda, although I did notice that there were no blacks at his meetings. I found the Gritz meetings very informative. They were a consciousness-raising experience. "Ohhh," I thought to myself. "There are things going on in this world you are not aware of! The world isn't always as it has been sold to you." That got through to me. Gritz emphasized taking the time to stay abreast of public affairs and I started to do that.

I moved back to Indiana to be near my family and went back to school and I was working, but despite a very busy schedule, I did what I could to keep up with what was going on in the world. One thing I did was subscribe to a publication called *The Aware Woman's*

Newsletter. It had a personals column, and that is how I met my husband. He and I never talked about race when we were getting to know each other. It was when we moved to Florida after we got married that he started talking to me about things he was reading in a magazine he subscribed to, *American Renaissance*. It was at this point that my racial consciousness light came on. From then on, it has gotten brighter and brighter.

I started to read some of the issues of *American Renaissance* that were around the house. There were articles about the extent of black-on-white crime and other things that were not being reported in the mainstream media. "Oh my goodness!" I thought. "The media and the government aren't telling us things!"

I've also started reading articles on the American Patrol web site and other sites. I asked myself, "Why aren't the mainstream media talking about the things these Internet sites are covering?"

As time went along, I reached the conclusion that the media are never going to talk about these things because there is a large governmental campaign of some sort that the media are part of. And what is that campaign about? Nothing less than an attempt to ruin the civilization white Europeans have built in this country. Maybe I'm tying too many things together and going overboard and being too radical, but that is what I think.

I was reading someone's views on a web site recently, and he talked about the mongrelization of the white person. I thought that was a good term for what is going on. We are being fed the idea from every quarter—movies, television, newspapers, everywhere—that it is OK to marry interracially and have interracial children. We are being told by the politicians that we should embrace all the non-white immigrants that are pouring into our country. We are being fed the line that everybody's equal and they aren't. Socrates and Aristotle were white. The people who developed penicillin and invented the airplane and the computer were white. White people can think. I know it is unfashionable to say that, but it is true. It gets me on my high horse the way the schools are rewriting history. It really gets to me that we can't point with pride to all the white geniuses. White people have been the victors in history, but now in school children go through these exercises where they are supposed to relate to how the losing side felt so, I guess, they will go over to their side. We are not going to stay the winners doing that.

We are losing touch with our heritage as a race, and I don't think it is just a matter of chance that that it's happening. I know this sounds radical, but I think there is an attempt to do no less than obliterate the white race. I read somewhere that white people are only eight percent of the world's population. I think there are people out there that would like to see us be no percent of the world's population. I think there is an attempt to dumb us down, soften us up, and interbreed us with blacks and Hispanics. Then, after a few generations, we'll be so stupid and docile we will do whatever the people in charge tell us to do.

As for the government we have now, I think it is a crock, a farce. The current president [George W. Bush] is a one-worlder. His take on it is that what is good for the immigrants is good for America. Hogwash. The Hispanics pouring into this country now, most of them illegal, are different from the European people who came here, in capability, in work ethic, in culture, and in race. Personally, I think Bush is just a front man, in front of the curtain, so to speak, posturing and pandering to the crowd. I think all the politicians report to some kind of New World Order group who is pulling the strings. I really do. I think we are being maneuvered into becoming one big globalized, mongrelized melting pot, and part of that is tearing down everything the white man has stood for and done in this country.

Whoever is behind the curtain, whatever group—and I don't really know who they are—is very powerful and very insidious and very deadly to the Caucasian race. With all their talk about justice and equality, they are taking advantage of the basic fairness of white people, who are of a kind to have authored the Mayflower Compact and the Magna Carta and the Constitution. We aren't savages and that has been cleverly used to hurt us, because we are accepting the pitch to be tolerant, be accepting, to be nice. The Mexican people flooding into the country and those who want to re-annex parts of the United States, the Reconquista Movement, they aren't playing fair, they aren't being nice.

It is as if we are rolling over and saying, "Rape me again." It's incredible. "Whatever you want, we'll give it to you: our homes, our schools, our jobs." Several states are talking about giving in-state college tuition rates to illegal immigrants. That's ridiculous. And even that won't be the end of it. They will hire Hispanic faculty, discriminating against white applicants in the process, and these faculty will teach students what the war in Texas war was "really" about and what they should do about it. English as a foreign language programs will have to be put in place, and "Whitey" will pay for them. The parents won't be able to afford the tuition, and Whitey will pay it. The students will default on their loans, and Whitey will pay them off.

Whoever is behind the curtain is really clever, I'll give them that. I find it fascinating the way multiculturalism gets us trashing ourselves. Its gotten us to go on and on about all the terrible things we have done in the past and are doing now. Multiculturalism gets us to accept, and even invite, minorities blaming us for every problem they have. We wind up looking after others' welfare and serving their interests while we ignore our own. That is really clever. They have it so that we can't say anything positive about our race, our heritage, our culture, because that is white supremacy, and we can't say anything negative about minorities because that is racism. This has all happened quite recently, because even when I was growing up it wasn't in place the way it is now.

Go to the American Patrol web site sometime. It is run by Glenn Spencer. His site is mostly on immigration, although it does touch a little on whiteness. He points out that since 1965, ninety percent of immigration to this country has been non-white. The American Patrol site is a daily account of the ludicrous. We are supposed to give amnesty to millions of immigrants, which will only encourage more illegals to come across the border. I read in Spencer's site that they are actually putting water tanks in the dry areas so that the illegal immigrants from Mexico won't get thirsty.

The question I ask of myself is, once they ruin all the things European people have built up in this country and it becomes just like the place they came from—poor infrastructure, no education, gutted economy, bad medical care, crime, and so on—where are they going to go then? There won't be any more European people to exploit.

I have been trying to stay abreast of things mainly through the Internet—governmental conspiracies, immigration, white nationalism, those areas mainly. And I talk with my husband and some of his friends. This has been going on for the last two or three years, and it has affected my perception greatly, and some of my choices in life. Even though I know that I am going to be vilified, if I am in a conversation that leans in the direction of any of these issues, I will make one or two leading statements. But I can't say they have any effect. I can't undo all the brainwashing people have been through. The people I come into contact with day-to-day find some movie star more credible on racial matters than they do me. Everything nowadays is glitter and glamour and fluff. There is no substance.

And I have to say I think women are more susceptible to what we are being sold. Put a morally high sounding and emotional spin on something and women will buy into it. That is how you sell them something. "Do it for the children"—tell them that. It will get them every time. But what women ought to be asking is at what cost, what is going to come out of this?

I am not involved in big crusades right now. I'm not in any organizations or anything or taking on any big projects. I'm trying to make my marriage work and get through school, and I have a clerking job to bring in some money, and that keeps me tied up. But there have been small, personal changes in me. I'm more aware now than before of where I conduct my business and where I live. I'm thankful we live a little bit out of town, and I think a lot about where we will live in the future. I am more conscious of my connection to the media. I realize, for instance, that minorities are portrayed as virtuous and in need. They have been done wrong, send money now. I notice how ads and television shows—especially UPN—show interracial relationships involving white women especially. I wouldn't have picked up on that before.

Except for my husband, I haven't found anyone to link with who shares my outlook. A few of my husband's friends think like he does, so that is helpful to him. Maybe I am missing some people I could relate to because I don't exactly announce my views loudly to the world. That can get you in trouble. My point of view is not something you want to wear on your sleeve. And if I did say something, most people these days are so busy and stressed they don't have time to think about anything but getting along day to day.

Where I grew up and my parents are still living, the black areas are still there, but compared to what it was like when I was in California, they aren't all that scary. You can drive through them on your way to some other destination and it's OK. I understand from my parents that the area has been heavily settled by Hispanics due to all the manufacturing in that area. To me, that is very sad. I see it as the disintegration of a good Caucasian area. My mother tells me that some apartment complexes that used to be all white are now all Hispanic and that they are unkempt. She says she notices the communication barriers in stores now.

One of the girls in my high school class married a black. My father saw her recently in town and she has three children. But that is an exception among the people in my hometown. That is in contrast to the large percentage of the population doing that now. I read in the paper today that a number of national companies are putting together marketing strategies specially targeted at mixed-race couples and biracial children because there are so many of them. Personally, when I am in Target or somewhere and I see a blond woman with a black man and mulatto children, I want to go up to her and ask, "Why?"

It breeds disgust in me to see what the people in charge of our society are doing. And what is even more disgusting to me is to see people accepting it. "Oh, it is so wonderful that we are all alike." No, we're not. No, we're not! Where I go to school now to get my masters degree, the classes are about sixty percent black. I can tell there is a difference in intelligence level—the blacks just aren't getting the material. I wonder how they are passing the program.

I'm hit with what is going on in this society everywhere I go. I have to deal with it where I shop, everywhere. I call an 800 number and get put on hold forever by someone with an accent I can barely understand and with an indifferent and vaguely hostile attitude. Bushes, trees, cats, and every non-white human on the planet is favored over me. It gets frustrating. Sometimes I envy the ignorant and happy people who have no clue about what is happening to our country and our race.

There is some fear in me about really stepping out and being heard and doing something. Maybe some of that fear is because I am a woman and I wouldn't be as afraid if I were a man, I don't really know. I know I would prefer not having my tires slashed or being shot at. Beyond that, I am a shy person. I'm just not a public person. I can imagine a day when I will be asked to put my finances, reputation, and life on the line and do what I can for the cause, but I don't know if that is the hill I want to die on.

I'm getting my masters degree in a few months and I would like to do work that goes along with my beliefs, but right now I don't see any possibilities along that line. As a practical matter, I have to earn a decent salary, if nothing else so that "Cleotis" and "Consuela" can live nicely. Those parasites are taking my paycheck! They are squeezing the white middle class out of existence! If I can find work that reflects my beliefs and values, that would be great. If not, I will find as good a fit as possible. When things aren't so hectic in my life, I hope I can do volunteer work in this general area.

My husband and I have talked about what we are going to do given the circumstance in the world. We always keep the option open of just going off somewhere to get away from all this. We could go to Wyoming or someplace like that, but like most people, we have to be within reasonable distance of where the jobs are. And there is the financial aspect of selling our home and all the logistics involved with relocating somewhere. There are a lot of roadblocks to get around. Ideally though, it would be good to live in a small community of like-minded people in a remote area. We would be with people we wanted to be around and we'd have support, and if things got really bad we could sell, trade, and barter among ourselves.

It would be good if I could say where I'll be ten years from now, but the truth is all of my life I have never seen more than one step in front of me. I think of myself as an intelligent person, and I ask myself, what is my problem? Although a lot of people I know don't know what they want to do when they grow up. There is a character in *Winnie the Poo* named Eeyore who all the time wails, "Oh me, oh my!" I'll never be like that. I'll always diligently shuffle ahead. I'll keep forging ahead in the fog holding a lantern up high. I don't know where I will end up, but things will unfold a little bit at a time.

4   LEARNING ABOUT BOOTY ON THE BUS

Mathew Rock is fifty and lives in Chicago. He teaches in a community college. He is married with two children. He has a whimsical manner.

I used to be a high school teacher, and I had a summer school teaching job in the summer of 1993, I think it was, and that was the first time I remember starting to think seriously about racial issues. I was teaching a class in world history. When you are teaching in the summer, you're pretty much working with kids who are the dregs of the student population; that's who's going to summer school. They aren't doing well, and they've got problems.

Anyway, I remember talking to another history teacher who was teaching another class and she had this handout and she said, "You might want to use this with your class." This teacher was Jewish, now that I think about it. I looked over the handout and it was about how the white race accidentally rose to ascendancy. I didn't say anything to this other teacher, but I thought to myself, what's this all about? I'm supposed to teach my students that it was just a mistake that the white race developed technologically and politically beyond the other parts of the world? What's going on here?

Another recollection, I remember a couple of years later and I was teaching computer technology in a community college—I had left high school teaching—and I had this guy in class who was a biology teacher in one of the local high schools. He was talking about how the latest trend was let's not make the curriculum Eurocentric. I was thinking to myself, we have all these freedoms and all the great things our people did, and I'm sorry if they were heterosexual white males, but that is just how it was, you know? This brainwashing of white kids that they are supposed to be ashamed of being Caucasian and understand everybody else—what is this business, where's this coming from?

I think a lot of the racial tension in this country is people aren't taught the truth about the world and themselves. We get across to kids that nobody is responsible for their successes and failures in life—somebody else is. Everybody is just as good as everybody else and it's circumstances that account for what you get in life. Now, I have a friend named Tom Chandler. I've told his wife that the reason Tom is more successful in life than I am is he smarter than I am. I could look at it in a Third World and minorities way and say I'm being held back and that's why I'm not as successful as Tom Chandler, but that would be ridiculous.

There was a movie about a high school principal at a black high school in New Jersey, Joe Clark. He was played by Morgan Freeman, the black actor. *Lean on Me*, I think it was. There was a scene where Clark addressed a school assembly, and he said, "We're here to raise academic standards." He said, "Don't go blaming the white man and don't go blaming your parents for your shortcomings." I think to a great degree the animosity of nonwhites toward whites is they think they have to find somebody to blame for their shortcomings. I have plenty of shortcomings. I am a hopelessly flawed creature and I'm not the equal of Tom Chandler, but I don't blame my buddy Tom Chandler for it. He didn't do it that he is smarter than I am, and he didn't prevent me from becoming a millionaire. That is just the fact of it, OK?

There is this theory in education that anyone can learn anything. Well, I'm sorry but I am not going to understand molecular biology no matter what you do with me. There's also something called multiple intelligences that's the big rage in education. Like the basketball player Michael Jordan who used to play here in Chicago; his athletic ability, they are saying, is a form of intelligence. Jordan was a great player, you can't deny that, but don't try to tell me that this man is intelligent because he can put a leather ball in an iron hoop. They aren't fooling us with this multiple intelligence business. We know what intelligence is, and some people have more of it than other people and Tom Chandler has more of it than I do, simple as that.

My wife is certainly less vocal and strident about racial matters than I am, but she was saying the other day, "Why don't I get to have a culture?" She was saying, "If an Irish guy lived next door to a Norwegian guy"—my wife's Norwegian—"and the Norwegian guy lives next door to an Italian guy, you mean that is not a culturally diverse neighborhood?" My wife has a point. The Irish and Norwegian and Italian cultures are different from one another. Their traditions are different. Maybe in the Norwegian home they speak Norwegian and in the Italian home they speak Italian. What's this idea that you gotta be from Third World countries or black to have a culture?

There used to be a T-shirt on college campuses that the black students wore that said, "It's a black thing—you wouldn't understand." If someone paraded around with a T-shirt that said, "It's a white thing—you wouldn't understand," there would be a furor over that. A few years ago, blacks wore baseball-type hats with an "X" on it, I guess in honor of Malcolm X, and I think the hat was pushing a movie about him. Then other people started wearing shirts with a Confederate battle flag on them that said, "You wear yours and I'll wear mine." You can imagine how that went over. Whites are supposed to keep any show of pride in their heritage under wraps. Malcolm X called whites blue-eyed devils, but it is just fine to wear a hat honoring him. But that's the way the rules of the game go at the present time. The question is who set up those rules and how'd they do it?

I don't know if I agree with a lot of stuff they do in Scandinavian countries—I mean, I'm not a socialist by any stretch of the imagination—but things work over there and it isn't because their system is so great. It's because they're a homogeneous culture, the people have a common thread, and it's because of the make-up of the people. You have capable people there. I remember about seventeen or eighteen years ago, the Bears [the Chicago Bears in the National Football League] won the Super Bowl and everybody was talking about the great system [assistant Bears coach] Buddy Ryan had—they called it the "46 Defense." Ryan said it wasn't the system, that it basically boiled down to the fact that the Bears had more talent than any other team that year. It's the people not the system, that's the point—and Norwegians are good people, good white people.

I firmly believe that the big reason America is one of the richest countries in the world is because we've been predominantly a country of European people. This country could be a melting pot and have it work because everybody who came here was from Europe. But now we have this bio-stir fry going and it's not going to work. Race is the basis of culture. Genotype [internally coded, inheritable impulses] shapes culture, and phenotype [outward appearance] is an indicator of genotype. What I'm saying is you can predict how advanced a country is going to be and how people are going to behave by looking at racial make-up. It isn't all a matter of circumstance or luck. We are being pressured to think race doesn't matter, but it does.

The World Health Organization has criteria they use to measure countries—the gross domestic purchasing power, life expectancy, literacy rate, and some other things I can't remember offhand. The point is you can lay that measure over the white countries and black and mixed race countries of the world and get a perfect fit: whites high, the others low. You're crucified if you even hint at white supremacy, but you can predict with a very high level of certainty what a place is going to be like just by looking at its racial demographics. If you don't believe me, look at what happened to every American city when its racial composition changed.

The United States is such a popular place to come to because of what the white settlers and the other European people built here. People aren't pouring into any non-white country. We're still a majority European country, but I have read that whites will be a minority by the middle of this century. I think Clinton said that, and I've read it other places. I won't be around then, but I bet at that time we are more like Brazil or Puerto Rico is now than America is now. I don't want to go so far as saying race is destiny, but it's close. That's what I think, and I fully understand how unpopular and condemned it is to think that way.

Chicago has the fourth biggest Hispanic population in this country. San Antonio and Houston, and maybe El Paso, I can't remember exactly—anyway, all places down near the border of Mexico, and then there is Chicago at number four. Chicago got established as a center for illegal Mexican immigrants. If you're asking me why, I don't know. My wife's theory is it's because the rich want an abundant source of cheap labor. She works in a school that used to be in a white working class area and now it's heavily Mexican. I agree with her about why a lot of Mexicans gravitated here. If the rich, or whoever is really in power in this country, didn't want these people here, they wouldn't be here. You'd have divisions of army at the border. They'd do something like tell the Mexican government you've got ninety days to stop it on your own, and if you don't, we'll consider illegal immigrants hostile forces and shoot to kill. Believe me, it would stop.

The news we get is managed, whether it is about immigration or anything else. When I was single, I dated a woman who worked for a local newspaper and she said that by the time something, let's say about race, gets into print, it gets fit into the official message regardless of what actually happened. Information in this country is controlled by a small elite, and if you don't go along with their agenda, you are represented as evil.

I have to admit the system of thought control works really well on white people, to the point that they turn on anyone who tries to talk about what is going on. We are the only people I can think of that come down on any among them who brings up anything related to their own well-being as a people. You know, a black person says, "Let's take a look at how blacks are doing," and other blacks don't go, "Shut the guy up." But a white person says to white people, "Let's talk about how whites are doing," and whites say, "Stone him, he's a Nazi!" We've been had.

Really, to a large extent we don't produce our own culture in this country. Hollywood does it with their movies and television shows. I remember the shows on television in the '50s. I'm not saying it was high art or anything, but I wouldn't have any problem letting my kid watch those variety shows and situation comedies. But it's just garbage now, MTV and the rest of it. Ugly, base, brings us down as a people. My theme is we have to start looking more at who is in charge of feeding us entertainment. Who are these people? Maybe it is Jewish revenge for the way gentiles have treated them over the centuries, I don't know. I don't advocate violence, but there could come a day where we barge into a Hollywood office like Marine raiders.

I believe a lot of the news and entertainment coming out of New York and Hollywood is propaganda. Like the media love to tell us how violent we are as a culture. You know, the United States leads the industrialized nations in murders and violent crime and so on. What they don't tell you is who among us is committing all this crime. You take out the minority crime and we are just like the Scandinavian countries or Belgium. White people commit just about the same level of crime no matter where you go. And that is also true of blacks—black crime rates here in this country are very much like black crime rates in African countries. High here, high there. But the mainstream media—and I'm including the book publishers, all of them—aren't going to bring that up. You might find out things like that from the Internet, but you aren't going to get it from *The New York Times*. That kind of information isn't in line with the program to get us to welcome minorities and all that comes with them into our homes and workplaces and bedrooms.

I have a nephew in his early twenties and he had a black girlfriend and he ended up marrying her and they had a child. This woman has turned out to be trouble and he has filed for divorce. Those of us who told him not to get involved with her in the first place were called racists. But I told him he failed to understand that the races have different ways of looking at the world and approaching things. He bought the idea he was getting in school and everywhere that we are all the same. We're running from the truth in this country, or maybe it's we're being led away from the truth. And it's cost my nephew big time. I mean, it is crazy—it's pounded into us. Some Hollywood actor in a movie will get up there and…I don't watch a lot of TV and I don't want my kids watching it, all these shows and these little ads for diversity. Personally, I've always believed that high fences make good neighbors. I know that isn't a acceptable idea these days, but I think it is the truth.

My wife was talking about her childhood and everybody was white and she said, "Forgive me, but I liked the way it was then better than the way it is now." I said to her, "What are you apologizing for? They got you apologizing." There's this pervasive message that if you want to be among your own and you're black or Hispanic or Asian, you're fine, but if you're white and you want the same thing,

Robert S. Griffin

you're a hater. They've got it painted that anybody who's proud of being white and wants to hang around with white people is, you know, a Nazi or something, or a Klansman.   That's patently ridiculous.

The problem now is us whites aren't racially conscious. We've been so conditioned to be "other race conscious" we don't see blue-eyed poverty and suffering, or we glance at it and move on. If you have ever been to Appalachia you know what I am talking about. Last night, I was watching this show on public television about Sun Records [in Memphis, Tennessee] and [its owner] Sam Phillips and the birth of rockabilly music [in the 1950s]. [Sun Records is where recording artists like Elvis Presley, Jerry Lee Lewis, Johnny Cash, and Carl Perkins got their start.] Every one of those guys with the exception of maybe one or two came out of sharecropper backgrounds. They were all blue-eyed white guys that grew up dirt poor.   Billy Lee Riley was one of them, although people don't remember him. He could have been big, but I guess Phillips decided to push Jerry Lee Lewis' record "Whole Lotta Shakin' Goin' On" instead. Anyway, nobody is going to tell me a lack of melanin and blue eyes means the world is your oyster, 'cause it's just not that way.

I got out of high school teaching for a while and was trying to get back into a Chicago high school, and the principal just came right out and told me that he had been told to hire a minority. Most of the time they do it but they don't say it. Three weeks later he gives me a call and says to come in for an interview, that he was having trouble finding a qualified black to fill this teaching position. I got that interview and then a second one. They were really candid with me. They said, you're more than qualified, but if we can find a black that we think can do the job without being so bad the roof caves in on us, that is what we are going to do. Well, they finally found a black and I didn't get the job. That does put me off, but more than anything I feel helpless. The ones who could do something about what's going on, the politicians, don't care about people like me.   They are a professional class to themselves and they are interested in their own survival, bottom line.

My kid is seven and rides a bus to school. We adopted kids late in life. I'm going to be sixty-two when this kid goes off to college.

34

Anyway, my kid is coming home and he's talking about booty and this and that and he's cussing left and right. He's obviously picking this up from the older black kids on the bus—where else does a little white kid get this stuff? It's one of the outcomes of diversity they don't talk about but we have to live with. My wife and I have talked about home schooling, but my wife would have to quit her job and that would be tough on us financially, and I don't know if she wants to stay home all day.

I see us white people shooting ourselves in the foot. It just seems like we accept whatever we are told. And it's like as long as we have our TVs and shopping malls and SUVs we aren't even going to pay attention to what's going on much less complain and do something about anything. I guess one thing is to get the word out to white people that, hey, just because your pantry and refrigerator are full doesn't mean things are good.

5   SWF SEEKS STRONG, TRADITIONAL WHITE MALE

An online personals ad read as follows:

I am a 30-year old, single white woman seeking a strong, traditional white man for family building. I am a racially aware Southern gal with Scotch-Irish/Swiss ancestry. I am a graduate of a four-year university but have recovered from the brainwashing. I have worked as a newspaper editor, play traditional Irish and Appalachian fiddle, and like to dance. I am a former county beauty pageant winner, 5'6", 120 lbs., blue eyes, and have long, red hair. I am ready to have an intelligent, physically fit Anglo man support me in my role as homemaker. I welcome correspondence from racially conscious men.

Margie O'Connor* lives with her grandmother in a small town near Winston-Salem, North Carolina. She has a soft Southern accent and gentle, sincere manner.

In high school, I graduated fifteenth in a class of four hundred. I was the homecoming queen and played three different sports—soccer, tennis, and basketball. I was most valuable player in soccer and tennis, and all-conference in all three sports. I had African American students on my teams and spent a lot of time with them. In those years, I saw myself as enlightened in that I was nonjudgmental about people who were black. Many other people I knew seemed to be pretending as though they didn't see black and white, but I saw their behavior as patronizing toward blacks. I felt as though I wasn't even seeing color and that I was treating each person as an individual. After high school, I went on to college and received a degree in psychology and worked as an editor for a newspaper for three years. I wrote several articles that touched on racial matters and some people implied that I was evil and hated black people and was one of those knee-jerk racists that Southern people are stereotyped as being. But I didn't come from that background at all.

Increasingly after college, I noticed things going on around me that began rubbing me the wrong way—the music that was blasting, television, movies, all the things that were being piped into our culture. It got to the point that it went completely against my grain. I was happy with my culture here—playing traditional music and going over to my ninety-year-old grandmother's house and hearing her talk about when there was no highway through here, and going over to my great aunt's house where she made quilts. I embraced what I loved around here and everyone else was talking about the next "Friends" episode and making $60,000 a year. Also, over the past five years there has been a big influx of mixed-race migrant workers here—they work in tobacco—and everything is bilingual now. That has been very disturbing to me.

Two years ago, a friend recommended that I read David Duke's book [*My Awakening*]. Reading that book, I saw that Duke isn't the ogre that he is painted as being. He is a very intelligent and thoughtful and sincere person who at a young age became committed to deal with some very controversial issues. He talked in the book about his childhood—he is Southern, as I am. I felt a kinship with his story. I thought, here is someone I can relate to. Here is someone who, when he was young, instead of getting involved with art or music or sports, got involved with social issues. David Duke's book helped me put words to what I had been experiencing. Reading that book was a real turning point for me.

About two weeks after I read the Duke book, it just so happened that he was scheduled to speak about thirty minutes from where I live here in North Carolina. That area has a lot of chicken farms and is around fifty percent Hispanic now. Not to get all mystical, but I saw his coming to my area as a sign. I went there and met him and got him to sign my book.

For a long time, I have been disenchanted with the idea of just having a professional career—being a career woman doesn't appeal to me. Duke's book has a chapter called "Women and Society," I think it is, and that helped make it all right for me to say, "I just want to stay home and play music and have a garden." My mother is on the big kick of me going back and getting my masters degree for some reason. She still doesn't get it.

Until I read the research Duke presented in his book, I was of the belief that there were no real differences between blacks and whites. I accepted the argument that any differences that we saw were a product of slavery and poverty and the lack of opportunity. If you were to suggest that blacks in Africa seem to have the same problems that blacks do here, I would have said that is was because of the harsh conditions in Africa. But Duke used the example of Iceland, which is a godforsaken place. The white people there have managed to turn it into a thriving economy and livable place. Duke compared Iceland to Haiti. Haiti is a virtual Eden, with ports and natural resources, yet it is like a cesspool.

When I go into town, I get accosted by black men on the street all the time. They make overt comments and just glare and look me up and down. I am now of the belief that that behavior is every bit as much a part of them as the color of their skin. I don't believe anymore that what they do to me is simply a product of their rearing. And I think there is a difference in intelligence, and in temperament, I guess that is the word for it. To me, an evolutionary argument to explain racial differences, or a good portion of them, is completely reasonable. Duke has a section in his book—not that he developed the material, but that is where I got it—that in human beings, like with any animal species, any trait that enables the species to survive is the one that will be selected. If you evolve in extremely cold conditions, that selects for different traits than if you evolve in an extremely hot, tropical environment. That just makes perfect sense to me. The Duke book goes through my mind whenever I see black people acting as they do.

When I was working at the newspaper, I went out on a limb a few times about the black issue. I cited some violence and rape statistics, and I know that gets controversial. Make the suggestion that black men are more violent and you are going to be called a racist. But you can't deny that they are committing these crimes and that it's not getting any better. I think it is best for the happiness of all races, not just the white race, that the races remain separate. I don't think there is going to be a peaceful world until all the races have their own separate spaces. There is a furniture market around here, and people from all over the world come here to it, to this little city. There is something enchanting about that, to see all the diversity in one place. But then I just want everybody to go home. It is ironic to me that those who praise diversity don't favor separating the races. Races living together encourages both cultural and physical interbreeding, and that dilutes the uniqueness of each race and blends away their diversity. Nature provides wonderful diversity, and then the diversity advocates take it away—it makes no sense.

I don't believe race-mixing [interracial coupling and procreation] is a good idea. Really, I have never been attracted to that. Actually, I think if they could peel off the layers of media and school propaganda, practically all white women would feel as I do. So many women I know are taking Zoloft and other anti-depressants. To me, that is a symptom that something is just not right in their lives. They are being conditioned by the media to go in directions, interracial dating being one of them, that aren't true to their nature and aren't going to bring them happiness.

The Duke book talked about how the media are basically Jewish dominated, and after re-reading that material and thinking about it, I have come to see that as a major part of the disease in this country. I'll give you an example: Country music has always been associated with the South and Christianity and people going to church, and it has always tended to be conservative. The country music station that plays videos never had any racy things on it, and on Sundays it always maintained respect for the day. CBS, which is Jewish owned, bought the station and now I see commercials for rap music. This past Christmas, they played a movie that had no Christmas theme at all. It had the most explicit sex scenes that I have ever seen on television.

I don't necessarily think that Jewish men are sitting around openly saying let's put these things on television and in the movies to force cultural norms on white people and completely corrupt their whole race so it makes it easier for us to control them. But I now see Jewish people as a separate race, and I have concluded that psychological traits can be as much a part of someone's being as physical traits. The direction Jewish people take things, I think, is just them, is just a reflection of who they are. And I think it is their strategy for survival and success and that they don't have to talk about it. They just understand it among themselves. Actually, I am in awe of what they have been able to do considering that they are only two or three percent of the population and yet control most of what people see on television, listen to on the radio, see in the movies, and read in books.

My younger brother is a victim of what is going on in this culture. He's 6'4" and has broad shoulders. He should be lifting things and working in the fields. But it seems that he, like so many white men, is distracted and—I don't know quite how to put it—softened, or domesticated, or emasculated somehow. People like my brother evolved from nature. Nature is in their souls. But they are losing touch with that. They are being taken away from things that are real and important to things that are not real and that are trivial. I'm talking about the kinds of lives they see portrayed in the movies and on sitcoms. Nothing disturbs me more than to see a group of white men watching an NBA game and spending all their time idolizing those kinds of people. On MTV, there is a show where they tour celebrity homes. My brother watches it. He sees these black athletes who have multi-million dollar homes and Rolls Royces. For white men like my brother, hardworking men struggling to have something for their families, it makes it seem like what they are doing isn't as important as what these athletes are doing. The media has made out athletes to be the big heroes of our day because they can put a ball in a net or run with a football. My brother watches that and is affected by it.

Also, all the explicit images you see everywhere now encourage men to think that if they are happy staying home with their wife and kids, they are uncool. If they aren't hooking up with their mistress on the weekend or going to the strip clubs, something is wrong with them. I think that white men who normally would be happy with a family and a home and having somebody to support them and encourage them feel pressure to do things that deep down they don't really want to do. But they feel the whole world is doing it, so what's wrong with them? They think they should be out doing the same thing.

I have some guy friends who, for certain, feel the same way about the race issue as I do. You can see it in their eyes when loud blacks drive by acting, to put it simply, crazy. But they don't really say anything. And here is where I see white women coming into this. I think white men suppress their views and their true natures about race because they know white women are going to be embarrassed and afraid that the men are going to lose their jobs. The white men know that the women are going to be worried that their friends are going to think, "She's married to a horrible racist." I can understand why women want to stay away from the race issue and the immigration issue because they insinuate hate, and women are supposed to be compassionate. Women like things that are pretty, and these can be ugly issues, that's true, and it is seen as even uglier when a woman speaks of these things than when a man does.

But nevertheless, women need to speak out about these things. If a woman loves her children, she needs to speak out. If she doesn't want them to be enticed into a base and alien way of life, she needs to speak out. If she cares about her children's physical safety and her own, she needs to speak out. If she cares whether her children become a minority in their own country, she needs to speak out. With the influx of non-whites into our land, we are losing our cultural identity and unity. White women should be repelled at the idea of our sacred space being turned into an Africa or a Mexico. They ought to be outraged that they and their children are not able to walk on the street without fear of being accosted or raped. Nothing is more important than women letting their men know they support them in dealing honestly with their feelings. At the very least, women can stop being barriers to men confronting this crisis in our lives.

I've quit the newspaper and am living with my grandmother. I'm building a small cabin on eight acres of land I bought five years ago. I have plans for a home I'd like to build, and I'd like a big garden. I've studied Jefferson's designs for Monticello for inspiration. To bring in some money, I do temporary work in Winston-Salem, which I'm not real happy with. Taking photographs is a hobby of mine. I'd like to get better at that. I started a novel a couple of years ago and I hope to complete it. The book is a Southern novel and somewhat autobiographical. The whole story is laid out and I have bits of chapters written. I've filled several notebooks full of paragraphs and ideas. Someday I would like to get a horse.

I have played and sung music professionally on and off for the past ten years. I've written lots of songs, but I've never done a CD of them. That is something I would like to do. You definitely have to look a certain way these days to be in the country music business, and I guess I have the right looks. I kind of have a problem with that, though. I mean, you heard me talking about what the media do, and now you hear me talking about wanting to manipulate the media to get my music played on the radio.

I'd like to travel more and I think the music would let me do that. I haven't traveled a whole lot. I've been mostly happy here. I dated someone from the time I was twenty to the time I was twenty-eight. I'm a curious and independent person, but I guess his company made me happy just to do simple things here.

I'd love to have a place that is isolated, with lots of animals and children around and with me free to do my creative things. I had a lot of love and support as a child, and that is what I have to give to the world. My life situation now makes it almost impossible to do any of these things I have talked about. I can't have the children; I don't have a husband. But even though right now I don't have what I want, it is comforting to me to know what it is. I could go on to graduate school or do whatever else I wanted to do, but I am in touch with what makes me happy. I have this picture in my head.

It's hard right now for me to say, "OK, I'm going to find a husband." I'm wary of going after it directly like that. I don't think that is how it works. I think I need to continue to do things that make me happy and he will be there on that path. I feel strange for the ad to be there. I didn't actually write it. My friend wrote it. He's known me for a long time. It was his idea. He's the guy I saw for eight years. I know that must sound very strange that he wrote the ad.

It isn't a natural thing to be living with your grandma when you are thirty as I am. But she is sort of a surrogate in place of not having a husband. She kind of fills that role a little bit and my mom does too, and I have friends. But really, nobody looks out for me or protects me. That may reflect a general lack of reverence for women nowadays. I think all women want to feel secure, that they are going to be looked after, that there is someone to take up for them. I guess it is just a primitive thing. You want somebody to be there to protect you, to beat up the bad guy. No matter how strong I might think I am, how much I go to the "Y" and work out, there are people who could overtake me in a minute, take me off and I'd never be seen again.

6   MORNINGS IN PHILADELPHIA

Bill Jordan*, fifty-three, lives alone in Philadelphia in a neatly kept apartment and works the night shift at the post office. His cerebral palsy has worsened over the years and he gets tired easily and his speech slurs a bit at times, but he is still able to make it to work every day.

Historically, there has always been a certain level of racial consciousness in this country—you know, a basic understanding that this was a country for white people—but I think most Americans have been nationalists more than racialists.   I know my primary identification growing up was as an American, that's how I saw myself.   From an early age, I felt a connection to the people who founded this country and the immigrants who came honestly here and blessed us with their presence and what they created for us.

It was in the 1960s when that started to change for me.   That's when I started hearing slanderous things from black militants about whites and race relations here in Philadelphia were atrocious.   It became clear that the black activists were talking about me, and that increased my sense that I'm not just an American, I'm white. I started to see that blacks felt connected to one another and that whites didn't feel that kind of connection. We see ourselves as individuals, or nationalities—Polish or Italian and so on—or as members of religious groups, or maybe part of some order like the Elks or something, but we don't see ourselves as a race with a common heritage and destiny. That detracts from our ability to defend ourselves and our interests when we are attacked by a group with a strong sense of commonality, whether it's the civil rights movement or anyone else.

During the 1980s I came to the realization that there was a Jewish consciousness and that Jews looked out for themselves first, ahead of the country or other people.   In 1985, I think it was, Jewish groups were upset that Reagan was going to Bitburg for the fortieth

44

anniversary of the end of World War II in Europe. [On May 8th, 1985, Reagan attended a ceremony at Kolmeshohe German military cemetery in Bitburg, Germany. One Jewish leader termed it "a callous offense to the Jewish people."] Reagan was trying to demonstrate the friendship that existed between this country and Germany, and I just thought that the Jews were putting their own interests ahead of U.S. foreign policy.

And there was a PBS program that I understand was Jewish produced that falsely claimed that the black 761st tank battalion had opened Dachau concentration camp. ["The Liberators: Fighting on Two Fronts in WWII" was aired on November 11th, 1993 on PBS and followed by a gala at Harlem's Appolo Theater.] I thought about that when I later read Kevin MacDonald's books [*A People That Shall Dwell Alone*; *Separation and Its Discontents*; and *The Culture of Critique*]. What I got from the MacDonald books was that the Jews had a campaign of extermination waged against them in the mid-20th century and they were understandably trying to make sure that it never happens again. So they are going to do everything they can to keep whites from being unified and in control. Promoting blacks and civil rights helps Jews accomplish that. It puts whites down and makes them feel guilty. It gets whites attending to the black cause rather than their own. Integration dilutes whites' culture by bringing black ways of living into it, and it decreases whites' connection with one another and whites' political power. And, with intermarriage, it even helps bring an end to whites' very existence.

In his last book, *The Culture of Critique*, MacDonald talks about the Frankfort School of intellectuals, all Jewish, who fled Germany in the '30s and came to this country. [The reference here is to chapter five of MacDonald's book, "The Frankfurt School of Social Research and the Pathologization of Gentile Group Allegiances."] They were the founders of cultural Marxism, or political correctness, that is undermining our way of life in America. This country gave these people refuge from their worst enemy and what do they do? They barely collected their luggage at the docks before they started subverting this country. But I suppose since they see us as an alien people they don't think they can commit a sin against us or against this country.

Jews don't want America to be a unified white country. That is why they are the biggest ones promoting open immigration. Jewish groups were very effective back in the 1960s when they lobbied to change the immigration restrictions we had established in the 1920s. [The reference here is to the Immigration Act of 1965 that greatly increased the amount of non-European immigration to this country.] The neighborhood where I live in northeast Philadelphia used to be about ninety-five percent white. Now we are being inundated with people from Pakistan and Mexico and all over. This area has drastically changed.

In Peter Brimelow's book [*Alien Nation: Common Sense About America's Immigration Problem*], there is a quote from a mainstream Jewish figure by the name of Earl Raab to the effect that "We're going to see that there are so many Third World immigrants in America that whites' power will be diminished and it will be safe for Jews." To me that is just infuriating. Ninety years after giving people like Raab refuge from the Czar over in Russia and one of them says something like that. But I have to give those people credit. They are getting the job done. From what I understand, according to the U.S. Census Bureau, the projection for the population of this country in the year 2100 is well over 500 million people, with probably twenty to twenty-five percent of them white. Kevin MacDonald said in his preface to the paperback edition of *The Culture of Critique* that there are four or five issues that we have to solve, but if we don't solve the immigration issue, we'll be inundated and our chances of solving these others will be cut off. Immigration is a particularly tough problem to tackle because big business wants it too.

If you'll notice, the Jews are big supporters of affirmative action, something else that decreases the influence of white gentiles generally and men especially. For instance—I think I have these numbers right—Harvard used to be eighty-five percent white Christian. Now it is twenty-five percent.

And Jews have been very prominent in the feminist movement, from Betty Friedan on to the present time. [Friedan's seminal book, *The Feminine Mystique*, was published in 1963.] You could even call it Jewish feminism and not be too far off. Feminism splits white women from their men. Men are seen as "them," the enemy, when white men and women ought to be working together. It gets women running after careers, and families and children suffer. I don't know if at the beginning feminism was meant to cripple white people, or even if that is the conscious intent now, but that has been the result. I'm just saying that if something brings white people down, look around and you'll find Jews.

Look, when [essayist and novelist] Susan Sontag says the white race is the cancer of human history, I have a right to try to figure out how many other Jews believe that, because they have immense power at the present time. Sontag makes commencement speeches and gets honorary degrees and nobody takes notice when she says something like that. Substitute "black" or "Jew" for white race in her statement and see what the reaction would be. There would be hell to pay. What Sontag said about whites is a genocidal thing to say. And what this Earl Raab said was genocidal, too, because when you displace a population you find it's harder and harder for white men and women to find each other as mates. And that could end in a slow genocide, a mixed race population. Do you see?

And don't think Jews aren't capable of mass murder and genocide. Lazar Kaganovich, who was Jewish, carried out the communization of the farms in the Ukraine in the 1930s where seven or eight million white Christians were killed in the process. We never hear anything about that, but it happened. Eighty to 100,000 Orthodox Christian and Catholic priests were murdered in the early 1920s in the Soviet Union. The Jewish-led Cheka, the secret police, was behind it, and most of its gunmen were Jews.

There is all this talk about anti-Semitism, but nobody talks about the anti-Christian fury among some Jews. Since the 1980s, *Commentary* magazine [published by the American Jewish Committee] has had articles saying Christianity provided the foundation for the Holocaust. Now, when you say a religion culminates in mass murder, what are you saying about that religion and the people who practice it? Look at how Christians are ridiculed in the movies and television now. Who do you think is producing those movies?

There is a wonderful book by Hillaire Belloc, who was an English Catholic political and religious commentator in 1920s. He wrote a book called *The Jews*. In it, he predicted a great cataclysm involving the Jews in the 1930s. And the reason was because of their involvement with Bolshevism. So Belloc predicted in general terms what happened in Europe in the 1930s. Of course, he's called an anti-Semite. But I've read the book and he doesn't blame everything on the Jews. He says that there's an incompatibility with Jews and Christians because of history, and basically that is the same thing MacDonald is saying.

I don't mean to imply that I think Jews are the only problem, not at all. Christianity is very much a part of the problem. It is such a universalist faith that, to a lot of people, to have any racial consciousness seems to be un-Christian. And just today, I read a quote from a Congressman who is well known for being on the forefront of opposition to attempts to restrict immigration. He has an Anglo-Saxon surname, which makes what he said particularly infuriating to me. Anyway, he was quoted as saying white people have no right to have racial pride. If anyone in this country has a right to have racial pride it's whites—you know, Washington, Jefferson, Lincoln, and all the rest. This culture was created by Mayflower Americans—that's in contrast to Ellis Island Americans—and they are the very ones that are being thoroughly demeaned in our colleges. Paul Craig Roberts, who's a syndicated columnist, says that the treatment of whites in this country is worse than the treatment of Jews was during the 1920s and '30s.

I read *Chronicles* magazine—that's my favorite. I was particularly heartened in the last couple of issues that Joe Sobran and Sam Francis [Sobran and Francis are also syndicated columnists] have taken on the *Commentary* crowd. Sobran pointed out that what Pat Buchanan called Israel's "Amen Corner"—[Charles] Krauthammer and all those people—immediately all got on the same page after the 9/11 attack saying that it had nothing to do with our close connection with Israel. Sobran said, "What are you talking about? For thirty years you told us that the Arabs hated Israel and wanted to push every Jew into the sea. They are obsessed with Jews, you said. And now this big thing happens and it has nothing to do with the Jews?"

Bush says that they attacked our buildings because they are jealous of our freedoms. It had nothing to do with our alliance with

Israel, he said. And he gets away with it. People buy it. Amazing! Bin Laden was very straightforward about what his problem was with us: our troops in Saudi Arabia, our sanctions against Iraq, and our support of Israeli terrorism against the Palestinians. Everything we have done in the Middle East has been to serve Israel's interests against the Arabs. Switzerland's a free country. Why didn't they go after Switzerland? Charlie Reese, the syndicated columnist, said that there's an old Yiddish saying that there's nothing thicker than a Christian's head.

It's beginning to dawn on white people—I hope, anyway—that that we have no leadership. Take someone like Jared Taylor [editor of the newsletter, *American Renaissance*]. First, practically nobody has ever heard of him. He gets to appear on radio talk shows every once in a while, and he got on the Donahue program when it was on cable, and very occasionally the *Washington Post* will give him a column. But the *Post* makes sure to line up six columnists to attack whatever he says.

Without an exception that I can think of, the white ruling class has no racial consciousness. They are a denatured bunch. Their main motivation is to preserve what they have. I think they have contempt for the average white person and have no problem making him a second-class citizen and discriminating against his children if it gets them ahead. The white politicians figure that the average white guy will never get off his couch and stop sucking on his beer long enough to make any trouble for them, and all they have to do to hold on to what they've got is keep the minorities calm with affirmative action and welfare and maybe even reparations some time in the future. If they thought it would keep them in power, they'd be fine with a million Mexicans flooding into Texas or California tomorrow. The few white politicians that do care about the flood of Hispanics across our borders would be hit with charges of racism—the cardinal sin of our time—if they tried to do anything, so they keep their mouths shut.

I think the Republicans have decided that Third World immigration has snowballed to the point where if they don't appeal to these people they're all going to vote Democrat. Peter Brimelow wrote an article in *National Review* magazine in 1995 or so saying that, with the big rise in the Third World population in this country,

Republicans won't be able win a national election from 2008 on. So the Republicans have come up with a Hispanic strategy assuming whites will keep voting Republican no matter what.

And it is not just that minorities are coming into this country in droves, it's the kind of people they are. They're people with a welfare mentality, if you know what I mean. They will vote for whoever promises to take something away from someone else and give it to them. So the Republicans have gotten more and more into that game. Although it's to be seen whether it is going to work for them, because it is really tough to out-promise a Democrat.

As for the Democratic Party, they are also getting more and more dependent on minority votes. Take my Congressman here in Philadelphia. He is dependent on Third-World votes to stay in office. Do you think he is going to bring up the fact that America is becoming balkanized? Not a chance. And anyway, the Democratic party is the home of deraciated whites. Either they have no racial consciousness or they have been so effectively conditioned they are actually hostile to their own people. I really believe that there is a suppressed—or maybe not so suppressed—hostility toward their own people among a lot of Southern whites. There is an old saying that there is no liberal like a Southern liberal. They are the kings at being guilt-ridden. People like Clinton and Jimmie Carter just wring their hands over the history of the South. A lot of people on the left consider the United States illegitimate because of the dispossession of the Indians and the enslavement of the blacks. It's not just a Jewish position. So they are on a kind of parallel track with the Jews, who are—I don't know how many people know this—the biggest contributors to the Democratic Party.

I think we have to pay more attention to the way the media deals with race. We all know about the dragging death of James Byrd, a black man down in Texas, by some white guys. [In Jasper County, Texas in 1998, three white men beat and cut the throat of James Byrd, a black man, before chaining him by his ankles to a pick-up truck and dragging him to his death, decapitating him in the process.] It was played up big by the media, I suppose to illustrate all the white hate crimes that are going on. A pamphlet Taylor's group [The New Century Foundation] put out shows that ninety percent of interracial crime is black on white, not the other way around. You'd never know that from watching television and reading the newspaper.

Let me tell you about a horrible racially motivated crime that was covered up. [In 2000,] a little white boy, eight years old, named Kevin Shiflett was standing in the front yard of his grandmother's house and a black man, yelling racial slurs, cut his throat. Now, the media does not want us to know about that hate crime because they want us to integrate with blacks, that's the program. And if we know what's happening, like Kevin Shiflett's murder, and all the statistics around assaults and robberies and murders of whites every year by minorities, and the actual number of white women raped by blacks and Hispanics every year, we might not be so ready to integrate with minorities like we are supposed to. One reason that Sam Francis is such a gem is that he reports things like the Shiflett case.

It's hard to defend yourself when you don't see yourself as a people, and white people don't see themselves as a people. Even if we did, I'm not sure we have the guts to protect our race and our place on this earth. I'm the son of a combat veteran in World War II, and I'm proud of my heritage. But I live in a country where the term brave white man is an oxymoron. Anglo-Saxons like me founded this country, but the mighty have fallen, or at least we are falling and falling fast. We're under siege as a race and we need to be together more, and we need leadership and we need to take action.

Maybe 9/11 will wake us up some, I don't know. We've had this tar-baby alliance with Israel for a half-century and it has gotten us all of her enemies. All the Arabs want from us is to sell us oil like they do every other country. They would have no problem with us if we weren't so tied up with Israel and supporting its attacks against the Palestinians. Back in the early '90s, we picked a fight with Saddam Hussein, who had not attacked America or any Americans but who just happened to be Israel's big enemy, and then Bush junior gets in and starts doing it again at the bidding of people like Richard Perle and Paul Wolfowitz. Sobran in one of his newsletters said that in the period when the Senate was deciding whether to approve the senior Bush's war, the American Israel Public Affairs Committee [a Jewish lobbying group] was all over Capitol Hill pushing for that war. And the same people—AIPAC and the neo-conservatives, almost all of them Jewish, like William Kristol, Norman Podhoretz, David Frum, and Jonah Goldberg—were banging the drums to go after Saddam again ten years later. Really, what happened on 9/11 was predictable, and if we keep doing Israel's business in the Middle East we'd better be prepared for something like that to happen again on our soil. The Arabs have proven they can, and will, hit us hard, right here in this country.

To be honest about it, I don't know what I can do personally about what's going on with race. Unfortunately, I have cerebral palsy, and it's been getting worse as I have gotten older. I want you to know that when I was thirty years old, or thirty-five, I was a pretty capable person. I work nights at the post office because I really have a hard time just getting up and going. I was married young and basically it didn't work out, and so I'm pretty much alone now. I've got a nice, comfortable apartment here that I rent. I sit here in the mornings before I go to work and have my coffee and read the newspaper or a book. I write my Congressman every once in a while and I try to talk to people when I can, like I talked to this truck driver the other day. But beyond that, it's difficult to know what to do.

7 "YOU'VE GOT A PALE FACE AND THERE IS NOTHING I CAN DO FOR YOU"

Steven Grant* is a twenty-nine year old attorney living in New York City. In manner, he is animated and quick.

I was born in San Francisco and raised in Kansas City, Missouri. I am the oldest of three children. My parents are both strong Christians. My father has been an active opponent of the death penalty. He has been a member of anti-death penalty organizations and goes to public protest rallies. Recently, I told him that I too am against the death penalty. I am against the death penalty for the white race. He hasn't offered a reaction to that comment.

My parents are liberal in outlook, but the home I grew up in was essentially apolitical in the sense that my parents didn't say "We're Republicans" or "We're Democrats." What I remember was them getting across the idea of the equality of all human beings. And it wasn't that my parents drummed that concept into my head. It was more like if, for example, Martin Luther King's name came up at the dinner table, we would all kind of bow our heads respectfully and say, "Ah yes, he was a great man."

The neighborhood I grew up in wasn't suburban really, but I wouldn't call it inner city either. It was just a pretty standard American neighborhood, with decent houses and well-kept yards and clean sidewalks. We had a lesbian couple living to the left of us and to the right was a married couple, senior citizens. A Jewish family lived "kitty-corner" across the street. About halfway through the time we lived there, a black woman moved in directly across the street. I remember there being some concern about that on the block, but it was pretty muted. I wouldn't go so far as to say I grew up on Sesame

Street, but it was fairly diverse where we lived. The neighborhood had a progressive political orientation. There would be fundraisers for the Democrats running for office, that sort of thing.

I went to college in the Midwest, and that is where I first got interested in conservatism. Looking back on it, just general contrariness may have had something to do with it, and maybe pity for the underdog. This was in early- to mid-'90s and political correctness was entrenched and conservatives were being dumped on. I remember reading [political and cultural satirist] P.J. O'Rourke's stuff in *Rolling Stone* and thinking, "Boy, this is funny. This guy has a fresh perspective. I have to look into this more." That led eventually to reading [economist Friedrich] Hayek and all the greats of conservative thought and checking out the Republican club on campus.

I got interested in journalism and majored in it and joined the staff of the campus newspaper. We had a minority affairs reporter—I think that was what it was called. He would faithfully cover every activity of minority students, every meeting, every speaker, every protest, whatever—the black men's student association, the Hispanic association, the gay and lesbian association, all of them. He would dutifully write what they wanted him to write. I wouldn't call it journalism exactly. This reporter was a good friend of mine and I'd elbow him and say, "What's the deal? You're a bulletin board for these people." It was fascinating to me how incredibly careful the paper would be around the issue of race, to the point that got funny at times. One time someone had used the term "black humor" in a column and a copy editor changed it to "African American humor." Even the faculty got a laugh out of that one.

I graduated with a degree in journalism and started looking for a job. I suppose you could say my real racial awakening came out of the fact that I had a lot of trouble finding a good one. I was hit with the reality that journalism is a virulently anti-white profession. The problem I was having getting placed was not due to a lack of skill on my part. I was much beloved by my professors. They thought I was great. I got A's in all of my classes. I was pulled aside by one professor who said, "Hey, you're the best one in the newsroom right now and I just want to let you know that." Another professor said,

"You are going to be a hell of a reporter." That made me glow inside. But the better internships—and internships were what we were looking for right out of school—did not go to white students. They went to black students, Hispanic students—anybody but white students. In fact, my advisor told me point blank, "Steve, you absolutely deserve a top internship, but you've got a pale face and there is nothing I can do for you." She said that matter-of-factly. I don't think she was saying "and I think that is terrible" or "that is a horrible injustice," or even "I think that's great, because we are increasing diversity and it is time for you white people to step aside." It was an unforgettable moment in my life to be in her office and hear that.

So there I was watching people go off to the *Washington Post* and the *Boston Globe* and the *New York Times*. I wound up doing an internship for a summer at the local newspaper, which was kind of disappointing and depressing. A friend of mine was half white and half Hispanic and he had the all-important Hispanic last name, so he got to go to the *Wall Street Journal*. It is not that he was bad, but I was a tad better.

After that summer internship, I headed out for Washington, D.C. to attend the Washington Center for Politics and Journalism, a journalist training program run by a guy who was a staffer to Paul Simon, the former senator from Illinois. In that program, you go to seminars and get put in news bureaus of newspapers. I went to the *Cleveland Plain Dealer*. That lasted about six months and I had a great time.

While I was in Washington I applied for a position in a program for new journalists at one of this country's best-known and most influential newspapers. I was informed that their program was exclusively for minorities and that no white people need apply. I finally landed a job at an Eastern newspaper as what they called a suburban correspondent. You didn't get the full reporter salary and you could only work there for two years and then you looked elsewhere for work.

My racial awakening continued on that job. Have you ever read the book, *Coloring the News* [by William McGowan]? That book gives a lot of examples of what I am talking about. Like you'd have a

Robert S. Griffin

good white journalist who'd been covering city hall for ten years and he wants the city editor job that he'd had his eye on for the whole ten years. What would happen is they'd hire a black guy just out of school, and within a year the black guy would get promoted to the city editor position. It would be a clear trumping of race over merit. A white American journalist is probably one of the more liberal species on the face of the earth, but even with that I'd hear white journalists talking out loud about what upset them about the affirmative action in newsrooms. They weren't going to write about it in the newspaper and they weren't going to go on the radio or CNN, but if you were at a party with them they'd say how much it pissed them off.

I had a black editor directly over me, a woman. She had previously worked at the *Washington Post*. She wasn't all that great. She clearly had her job because of her skin color. We had a couple of black and Hispanic reporters, full-fledged reporters, who amounted to minority cheerleaders. They'd write a story about the Cinco de Mayo festival and there would be pretty pictures of people dancing and that's it. And yet here they were in their positions.

About halfway through the time I was at that newspaper, they hired a black woman into the program I was in. The guy who ran the program was a genius-journalist type, Harvard educated, a brilliant guy. He hand-selected all the people for the program, but they did an end run around him with this woman. The paper sent a black editor, all expenses paid, to a job fair for an association of black journalists conference with orders to bring back a black person. And he did. And she was absolutely atrocious. She was barely able to spell her own name.

When this woman arrived, she said that she had had $15,000 in cash stolen from her on the train and that she needed some financial help to get started. Everybody is immediately suspicious of the story, including some of the black journalists. Who carries $15,000 with them in cash on a train? But nobody openly says anything about it because that would be rude. But the whispers start. So she arrives and people gave her money and somebody in the newsroom helped her out with housing by arranging the sublet of the apartment of a friend of hers. So she's got money, a place to live, and a car.

And she did nothing on the job. She would come in when she felt like it. She wrote virtually no stories. A lot of time, she just talked on the phone. She didn't produce at all, and before you knew it she was gone. She just disappeared, stiffing the subletter on the rent, by the way. I thought to myself, what an incredible injustice that was, because I knew how many applications the guy who ran the program got from white people he had to turn down because of sheer numbers. And here was this place made for this black woman who had demonstrated absolutely no merit whatsoever, who then blindsided everybody and seem to get away with it.

Midway through my two-year stint as a suburban correspondent, people in the program were starting to look for permanent reporter jobs. I decided to go to law school. It would be an exaggeration to say that the racial issue was what prompted me to go to law school, but it was high on the list. I applied to law schools in New York City for no other reason than it seemed like an interesting place to live and it is the legal and financial capital of the world. I got into what I would describe as a mid-tier law school—it isn't Harvard Law School, but it isn't the University of Guam School of Law either. I settled in for the three toughest years of academic rigor of my life.

I was concentrating so much on my law studies that I wasn't thinking much about the racial issue, but I did notice that no black or Hispanic students made the law journals and none of them were anywhere near the top rank in the class. But at this point I'm still thinking that probably the reason for their poor performance was racial discrimination. You know, they grew up in a tough neighborhood and that's the explanation for why they aren't doing well in school.

I graduated from law school and got a job in New York as an attorney. This is about a year ago. Just about at that same time, I was just fooling around on the Internet and stumbled onto a book called *Why Race Matters* by Michael Levin. He is a professor at City College of New York. I ordered it online and it turned out to be quite an eye-opener. This was the first book I had read on the whole topic of race. Levin talked about racial differences in intelligence and disposition. As I read, my eyes got wider and wider as I was seeing scientific proof for some of my suspicions. I started to think, "Wow, this is incredible!" You never see anything about racial IQ differences on television. You don't read about them in the *New York Times* or the *Wall Street Journal* other than to see the idea denounced as terrible and racist and hateful. Levin's book was what got the ball rolling around race for me.

Soon after I read the Levin book, I signed on to—drum roll please!—Stormfront, which is a web site run by a guy named Don Black. Black had been on "Nightline," so I found out about his site that way. Stormfront is sort of the wild frontier of white nationalism. A big variety of people post things there, from those who are barely literate to those who liberally quote Nietzsche and even more obscure philosophers. I signed up using my own name. I was one of the few people who didn't use an alias. Every once in a while I go on that site. I have read David Duke's book, *My Awakening*, and found that very informative. I found out about Jared Taylor's organization, American Renaissance, which has an Internet site [www.amren.com] and read the book he edited, *The Real American Dilemma*, and I took out a subscription to his magazine, *American Renaissance*. I was planning to go to the last American Renaissance conference in Washington to see what it was about and meet some people, but work commitments got in the way.

After this year of reading and thought, my manifesto, if you want to call it that, is, simply, white people do exist. They are a group with unique genetic characteristics. What they are is not just a function of being socialized in a certain way. They have legitimate group interests that should be furthered through social, legal, and political means. This includes—and here is where it gets controversial—the right to advance those interests by excluding people of other races, and not just doing that socially but using government mechanisms to accomplish that end.

To put it simply, we white people have a right to live and work among our own. If you look at the way people throughout the world have lived since time immemorial, you'll notice that they have clumped together by race. Now we are being conditioned to believe that when people do that it is evil. It's base, so we are told, and chauvinistic and wrong. What we ought to be doing, so the current pitch goes, is breaking down barriers and integrating here, there, and everywhere. But this simply is not what people want to do. They feel happier and more comfortable with people who look and sound like they do, and they have a better life that way. I think living with your own kind is as natural as trees growing and water running downhill.

My work as an attorney takes me to the Bronx. I must say, my great fear is that someday the whole United States will come to look like the Bronx. If that happens, it will to be soul death for white people. I walk through streets and tunnels that are urine-soaked, and there's chicken bones everywhere and graffiti, and the people walk by with their gold chains and their "do-rags" and their music blaring...and they are not my friends, they are not people I talk to, and I don't think that is because I am a terrible person or that I just don't know how to relate to them. I think there is something more basic going on, something more biological, more anthropological, that explains why I am not connecting with these people.

I don't think these people I see in the Bronx are inherently bad people. My belief is that, hey, when people are different and they don't get along, maybe there should be some distance between them. And maybe that is not such a bad thing. I mean, when two people are dating each other and they decide they aren't compatible and they need to break up, that isn't cause for protesting in the streets. Nobody sees that as an injustice. Nobody sees it as an injustice if a woman declines to date me because she just doesn't like something about me. And yet on a broader social level we consider it an injustice that white people don't want to live and work and eat and sleep and play with black people or Hispanic people.

Not only aren't white people disposed to looking at themselves as having group racial interests, they think the very idea of it is evil and something that they can't even go near, that it is "radioactive." The percentage of white people in the United States at the present time with a racialist perspective is very small. It seems to me that nothing is going to happen, on a large scale anyway, until a critical mass of white people are convinced on the issue. So that would be the starting point: spread the word, try to recruit people to a different way of looking at racial matters.

Or maybe it will take circumstances to awaken their consciousness—like white people getting inundated with minorities and everything that comes along with it. Yesterday, a black man burst into a bar in the Village [Greenwich Village] armed with guns and knives and gasoline screaming he was going to kill white people. He tossed the gasoline all over the bar and shot three or four white people. The cops subdued him before he could light the gasoline and do any more damage. They found some writings on him that said the white race has to die or something to that effect. The more incidents like that, the more average Joe and Mary Whiteperson are going to say, "Hey, wait a minute. That's wrong. That shouldn't be happening. There is no reason we should suffer things like this in the name of diversity."

Maybe it will take some sort of watershed event to wake people up, some kind of racial policy or action that is so detrimental to us that…although I don't know what that might be. It seems that white people roll with whatever punch hits them, whether it is getting belittled or discriminated against in jobs and school applications or having their neighborhoods ruined or being assaulted and raped and robbed, so I really don't know what it would take for us to say we have had enough.

As for what would happen if whites do become more racially conscious, I'd like to think that there can be peaceful legal and political ways to get what we need. Might it ever come to a violent confrontation, a race war? I am not a violent person. The idea of bloodletting certainly isn't something I relish. But it could be that the issue is so important…well, in this culture we certainly don't rule out warfare, per se. We haven't hesitated to send troops and warships and fighter jets to kill human beings in foreign countries to get access to oil or whatever. For me, a fight for racial survival is a more noble purpose than oil. So while violence isn't something I find appealing, if the stakes are high enough, I think we would have to consider it.

I was just sworn into the practice of law this past year. I would like to use my legal knowledge and skills to serve a grand purpose related to the race. That would be very satisfying to me. Litigating "tripped and fell" lawsuits doesn't excite me, but the idea of doing something for the white race does. I'd like race to be a focus in my work. Perhaps besides legal work I could write and publish or do public speaking. At this point at least, I don't have a master plan. I am just going to step out there and see where things go.

I have a girlfriend I met in law school. I talk to her about racial matters. At first she was shocked by what she was hearing from me. She is in the stratosphere in terms of intelligence and is always willing to embrace a bold idea, and so she listened. She and I recently read Pat Buchanan's book, *The Death of the West*, together and shared our reactions to what he had to say. She's told me, "I've been thinking about what you've been saying on the subject of race and I'm trying desperately to refute you, but I can't think of any intelligent comeback."

I know she definitely has a concern about this whole racial thing as it affects us. We have talked about how serious a matter it is and how the world doesn't want to hear about the kinds of conclusions I'm coming to. Our differences on the racial issue could be a divider, I can see that. I care very deeply about her, but I feel strongly enough about this issue that if she drew a line and said, "All right, you can have these beliefs about the white race and so on, but if you ever go public with them, if you ever write an article or speak to a group or join a group or something like that, then I would have to call it off between us," that would put me in a tough spot. I don't think she would ever do that, but right now I can't say for sure.

I sometimes wonder if I would have come to white racial consciousness but for having moved to New York City. The atmosphere here can be so brutal and loud and ugly and offensive. I don't want to continue to live in New York City. My girlfriend and I haven't talked concretely about marriage, but we have talked about places where we would be happy living someday. We agree that we don't want an urban environment. We want a suburban or rural environment. And I want a white environment. When I go to a white area it is like a cloud lifts. There is such a drastic difference. I'm struck with how peaceful and clean and nice it is compared to where I am living now.

8   TO RHODESIA AND BACK

Joseph Bishop is a bookstore owner in Washington State. He is forty-seven and married with three children. He has a quiet, serious manner.

The whole of western civilization is being brought down because of matters related to race, and yet we—white people—give little or no attention to racial matters as they affect us, our circumstance, our well-being, our future. When we attend to race at all, we primarily focus on how something or another affects other races, but only secondarily, if at all, do we assess its impact on our own race. Simply, we are not very racially self-conscious or self-concerned.

A conclusion I have reached is that virtually everything that has had or is having a racially negative effect on white people is furthered, if not initiated, by Jews. It's almost as if Jews have a collective consciousness in a Jungian sense that leads them to wage war on the gentile world. There seems to be something deeply rooted in their psyche and reinforced in their upbringing and culture and social connections that propels them in this direction.

Race as it relates to the well-being of whites and the connection of Jews to that concern: that is the fundamental issue of the age for white people. And tellingly, the most important issue of our time is the very one that we are most strongly discouraged from addressing publicly or even privately. With America as it is at the present time, we do so at our peril.

Like most people, I believe, I grew up with an awareness of racial differences. Despite the barrage of egalitarian rhetoric, white people, deep down, sense that the races are different from one another. For example, it's patently obvious that as a group blacks are not very smart, they're unpredictable, they're violent, they're dangerous, and their behavioral patterns are different from whites'. One does not have to be a committed racialist or possess a deep level of biological and sociological understanding to perceive this reality.

From a young age, I wanted to understand the significance of the racial differences I was observing. What does it mean to have a large population in this nation—blacks—that for all practical purposes is a dead weight on the rest of us? I first began to get involved in what I would later call racialism when I was around fifteen or sixteen. This was back in the 1960s. I started reading and associating with others of like mind, and that process has continued to the present time—over thirty years.

Back then, I read some of George Lincoln Rockwell's books. [Rockwell was the founder and commander of the American Nazi Party. He was assassinated in 1967.] *This Time the World* was one of Rockwell's books I read, and there was *White Power*. I think you can still get them through public or university libraries. Librarians can obtain them through interlibrary loan if they don't have them in their collection. Or at least they can with *White Power*. I'm not sure if *This Time the World* is available. I was a regular reader of a journal Rockwell published, *National Socialist World*, and similar periodicals such as *Western Destiny*. I think if you dig around with the help of a reference librarian you can find these publications. Another book from the 1960s I found useful was Carleton Putnam's *Race and Reason*.

I also studied National Socialism in Germany. Here was the first race-based society in modern times that tackled the problems that I had come to see, particularly Jewish power. And I am not referring to what has come to be called the final solution. I'm talking about the way National Socialists viewed race, how they made it central to their personal and collective existence, and the way they took on the negative influence Jews were having on German society at that time. I read George Mosse's book, *Nazi Culture*. Mosse's book is a survey of the intellectual and cultural life of Germany during the Third Reich. Even though Mosse is hostile to National Socialism, the book is a fine one and it gave me insight into how one government, one state system, appreciated the racial problems it faced and resolved them.

In the early 1970s, I worked with Dr. [William] Pierce's group in the Washington, D.C. area. It is now the National Alliance, but back then it was called the National Youth Alliance. I then spent twelve years in Africa. I went to Rhodesia in the mid-'70s as a volunteer. Rhodesia was waging a war against black terrorists who were murdering white people in the countryside. Rhodesia had a small white minority who was struggling to retain power in white hands. Racialists in this country took an interest in this, and I was one of a very few that actually went there to join the Rhodesian army and take part in this racial struggle, this racial war.

What I found in Rhodesia was a beautiful country and a white population that was overwhelmingly racially conscious, racially positive, and united and committed to doing the right thing: keep power in white hands. The Rhodesian Prime Minister, Ian Smith, was one of the few politicians in this world who was honest, upright and decent. It was a remarkable experience for me to be there—I was only twenty years old. I felt that I had a purpose and that I could directly assist my fellow whites. I served as a regular in the Rhodesian Land Infantry. At first I was assigned to a combat unit. Mostly we patrolled looking for terrorists. Later on, I was put into an intelligence section and did things like interrogation and compiling reports.

Ultimately, of course, the country passed into black control and is now called Zimbabwe. I stayed in the country for a few years and watched it decline. Once power shifts into black hands, decline is inevitable and irreversible. I went to a university in South Africa and majored in ancient history and German, although I didn't get my degree. I married my wife, who is a Rhodesian. Now, sadly, Zimbabwe is basically a toilet and whites are being murdered by mobs of blacks in alarming numbers.

Since returning to the United States, I have tried very hard to live in accordance with my deepest convictions about race and what I believe my life means. My wife and I have three daughters, eleven, nine, and seven. We educate them at home. We don't want them to absorb all the politically correct nonsense that the schools shove down the throats of children today. We want them to be raised with a definite white identity. We want them to understand race and its connection to civilization and to understand who they are and why it's important that they appreciate their heritage and perpetuate their race. And they do understand that, even at their young ages.

We have our children tested academically on an annual basis, and all three of them post high school level test scores. Apparently that's typical of home-schooled children because they are being given a good basic education instead of the dumbed-down curriculum they would be getting in a public school. We teach them how to read and all the math subjects and geography and basic science and so on. And we also teach them about race. They understand that virtually everything worthwhile that they appreciate and enjoy is the creation of white people. They understand what will happen if white people disappear—all these good things will also disappear. We hope that they will develop a firm racial identity and marry other white people and make racially positive choices in their lives.

Since I returned from Africa, I have done a lot of reading about race from a scientific, biological perspective. Philippe Rushton's book, *Race, Evolution and Behavior*, has been a particularly important reading. [Rushton is a professor at the University of Western Ontario in Canada. In his book, he offers evidence that East Asians, Europeans, and Africans differ, in descending order, in brain size, intelligence, sexual restraint, law abidingness, and social organization.] For anyone who is interested, the Scott-Townsend publishing company has a good list of books of this sort.

I have rejoined the National Alliance, and I have become very interested in historical revisionism. [Historical revisionists focus their attention on World War II in Europe and challenge the conventional interpretation of that conflict, including the accepted account of the Holocaust. The major organization reflecting this orientation is the California-based Institute for Historical Review (IHR).] There are various revisionist publications such as the *Journal of Historical Review* [an IHR publication], which has contained a great amount of excellent material over the last twenty-five years. I've become involved with the IHR and have tried to help it along. I've also been active on the Internet and in my community with neighbors and friends. I try to reach people, a lot of times informally—I just talk to them. Important issues can come out in everyday conversations. If you do it in an intelligent way, you can guide people toward racialism, or at least away from the standard avenues of political correctness. If I thought I could reach a half dozen people a year and get them involved in racialism or at least more interested in it, I'd feel as if I had accomplished something.

I realize that it is a very sensitive topic, but I believe strongly that whites need to come to grips with the inordinate amount of power and influence Jews have in the Western world, and with the fact that Jews are using that power and influence to deconstruct our civilization and our race. I don't consider Jews to be white. Racial identity goes beyond the purely biological. I see Jews as a separate "race of the mind": a mindset, an attitude, that is partly racial, partly spiritual, partly cultural, and partly political. Whatever they say publicly, Jews do not consider themselves to be white. Of course, I am talking in general terms. There are exceptions. But when Jews forge alliances with other racial groups, blacks or Hispanics, say, it is part of their war against "them," white people, gentiles.

It seems that Jews are the driving force in all of the things that weaken and destroy our race. You can't understand the black civil rights movement, for example, and the overall effort to get whites to intermix with blacks and defer to their interests unless you come to grips with the deep involvement of Jews in this movement from the beginning, whether it was being central in the founding of the NAACP and, until recent years, serving as its president, or Stanley Levinson writing Martin Luther King's speeches. If you accept the Jews' "equality" and "justice" rationalizations and don't see their support of black activism as part of a Marxist attack on private property and freedom of association, you are missing the point. If you don't comprehend Jews' push for an integrated society as an attempt to dilute white culture and solidarity and to literally destroy the white race through miscegenation, you are missing a fundamental reality.

There are many racialists who can't come to grips with the overwhelming and remarkable fact that Jews, this tiny minority, can have so much influence and be so destructive. But the truth of the matter is that Jews are the prime movers in every insane "ism" that is destroying our culture and civilization and race. Whether it is egalitarianism or feminism or multiculturalism, you'll find a disproportionate percentage of Jews involved in it. And underlying all of these ideologies, all these movements, is a Marxist frame of reference. For example, the whole approach of most of the leading Jewish feminists has been Marxist. Richard Pipes, who is on the faculty at Harvard, has written a very good book called *Russia Under the Bolshevik Regime*. I recommend Pipes' book to every racialist. He goes into the Jewish activity in the Soviet Union in the 1920s and '30s, which remarkably parallels what they have been doing in this country in recent decades.

An example of Jewish influence is the Frankfort School of intellectuals. Virtually all of them, if not all of them, were Jews who followed the same basic line their fellow Jews were taking in the Soviet Union. [The members of the Frankfort School of Social Research fled Germany in the 1930s and came to the United States and centered their activities at Columbia University. Prominent among them were Theodor Adorno, Max Horkheimer, Erich Fromm, and Herbert Marcuse.] The Frankfurt School wanted to transform society along their own racial, egalitarian, and Marxist line of thought. Their writings are the basis of all the currently fashionable movements in the society. So what is going on now isn't really all that modern. In fact, you can trace this kind of thinking and activity back into the nineteenth century—Jews were promoting these same evils back then.

Another example of what I am talking about is Franz Boas, who was Jewish and a professor at Columbia University during the first half of the last century. Boas promoted the egalitarian, and false, idea that all human beings, all races, are fundamentally alike and that circumstances make us what we are. He was kind of the father of cultural anthropology—Margaret Mead was a student of his. Boas was very influential in the decline of evolutionary and biological thinking in the social sciences and in using race as an analytical category.

Feminism has been one of the most successful forms of Jewish activity. Virtually all of the modern feminists, from the early '60s on, have been Jewish. The big problem with feminism centers around the way it has shaped women's perceptions of personal empowerment. Jewish feminists have sold the idea to women that they are not personally empowered unless they're pursuing a career, have few if any children, and delay childbirth if they do have children. The feminist notion of woman's absolute equality with their husbands has smashed families and devastated our birthrate. Our birthrate is our racial future, and the white birthrate has never been lower. If it continues as it is, we are on the way to extinction in a few hundred years—an instant in time historically. How many million white children have never been conceived because of Jewish-propagated feminist ideas? How many million perfectly healthy white babies have been aborted? How many marriages have been smashed up, or never occur, because of feminist propaganda?

I don't think we would have an immigration problem with the flood of Third World people pouring into our midst if our birthrate had remained healthy. We would have a United States with probably another hundred million white people than we have now. Fundamentally, the immigration problem is other races filling a population vacuum. We have an aging white population, and all these nonwhites flooding into America and other Western nations are basically filling the labor pool. Racialists have been very willing to take on the immigration issue, but they have failed to see that it is a consequence of another, more fundamental, problem.

I've been reading Michael Levin's book *Feminism and Freedom*. Levin, who is Jewish himself, makes no mention whatsoever of the disproportionate number of Jews involved in feminism. I had an e-mail exchange with him about this. I said to him, "How can you write a book about feminism and not mention all the Jews involved in this evil thing that has done so much destruction to our race?" Levin's reply was, "Well, what you say is true, but I really didn't want to get into that subject." He doesn't want to get into that subject, and that is understandable. But I want to get into it.

Feminism is probably the biggest evil ever imposed on our race. Yet few racialists are willing to talk about it. Some have confided to me, "We shouldn't talk about feminism because we need to enlist more women and we don't want to upset them." So they say nothing. That's insane. Serious racialists—and that includes racialist women—have to face all of our issues head on and be forthright about it.

Homosexuality is another terrible burden on our birthrate, and Jews have been very supportive of it. Very few homosexuals have children. Homosexuality is like a disease spreading through the society. How many millions of white people have been destroyed this way or, another way to put it, racially neutralized?

As for multiculturalism, the big push in schools at all levels, it is just more Jewish inspired craziness. Each race should immerse themselves in its own culture and history. I make it clear to my children that there are other people, other cultures, but that they need to understand their own culture, their own race, first. They need to understand and appreciate who they are and where they came from and where their people are going, because that is their identity and that is what roots them and gives them dignity and strength and purpose.

It is understandable that we don't acknowledge the reality of the Jewish problem—getting smeared as an anti-Semite and so on—but if we don't comprehend the Jewish underpinnings of the racial problems we face, how can we ever possibly hope to resolve them? I'm not saying we have to shout it from the rooftops, but it is something we need to face and be willing to talk about among ourselves and with others. The Jewish issue is not something we should be hiding or misrepresenting because doing that seems to be a clever way to advance our cause. We need to be honest and upfront about it. That's why I admire an organization like the National Alliance and Dr. Pierce. When he was alive, he was absolutely candid about Jews. He never compromised on this issue. He never retreated from this reality. I respected him for that.

I think it is possible to be forthright about the Jewish question without alienating people if we discuss it intelligently and rationally. Unfortunately, some of the people calling themselves racialists deal with this in a very kooky way, and that deters a lot of white people from involving themselves with racialism. Besides the whole mindset of Jews being innocent victims, the big problem trying to talk about Jews is that people see you pushing a nutty conspiracy theory and write you off. But the fact is that some Jewish activity is what could be called a conspiracy. Jews do get together at meetings of the Anti-Defamation League and World Jewish Congress and elsewhere to plan how to enforce their agendas on the world. On the other hand, you have Jews in the media and business and the arts and politics that seem to operate as individuals but nevertheless promote the same agendas as the organized Jews.

Recently, someone I respect suggested to me that, as Jews see it, crippling or destroying whites is a matter of self-defense. They have the suspicion and fear that whites are either anti-Semitic now or will become so at some point. He may have a point. It might explain why Jews work so hard to deconstruct Christianity, because they see Christianity as a unifying force for gentiles. They might believe that the Christian church, particularly the Catholic Church, has been used to combat them in the past, and that it could be an obstacle to achieving their agenda in the future. It does seem that no matter how far organized Christianity bends in their direction, Jews are still dead set on debunking and crippling it. All these court cases about Christmas displays in the schools and all; they aren't really about the separation of church and state. It is Jewish intellectuals and activists attempting to de-Christianize the United States. Virtually every sadistic killer on television and the movies has a crucifix dangling from his neck. Every priest is a weakling or a pervert. Don't think that it is coincidence. Have you ever seen a sadistic killer in one of those shows with a Star of David around his neck? No, and you probably never will.

And how do white liberals come to their own mindset on these issues? To a large extent, it comes back to the influence of Jews. How many liberals have sat at the feet of Jewish professors in the academy? How many of them have absorbed the politically correct message of the mass media that is dominated by Jews?

The Institute for Historical Review is an organization that understands the need to study Jewish power. Its focus for the last twenty years or so has been on World War II and the Holocaust. One could ask why is the Holocaust so important. Why do we need to focus on that? The reason is that, for Jews, the Holocaust legitimizes the "anti-Semitism" sledgehammer they use to pound anyone who opposes them into submission. They have it set up in people's mind that any criticism of Jews or any opposition to what they want equals anti-Semitism, which in turn equals the Holocaust. You don't like the level of aid we give Israel or our support of its campaigns against the Palestinians? You are an anti-Semite and, by implication, insensitive to the events of the Holocaust or actually sympathetic to it. "You are an anti-Semite" is a very effective weapon because white people hit with that immediately start retreating and pandering to their accusers.

The Holocaust-grounded "anti-Semite" epithet has been a terrific enabler for the Jewish agenda. That's one reason why it's so important to examine the events of the Holocaust and find out what really happened during that time. If the Holocaust story is riddled with lies and distortions—and it is—it helps remove this bludgeon, this weapon, and, it is hoped, will encourage white people to stand up to these various Jewish agendas. Also, we need to understand exactly what kind of Jewish activities led Germans to turn on them in those years. Why specifically was there so much dislike and hatred of Jews in Germany? It wasn't just some sort of irrational impulse as the Jews would have us believe. If we look into that question, we might come to understand better how Jews operate.

Historical revisionists need to find a way to reach more people. The average person only gets to hear the official version of what happened in the past. Historical revisionists need to examine more issues than World War II and the Holocaust. They should investigate the things I have been talking about here: the predominance of Jews in Marxism and Leninism, and the Jewish role in promoting all the trendy ideas in American culture, feminism, multiculturalism, multiracialism, cosmopolitanism, and homosexuality (which includes declaring anyone critical of homosexuals diseased, "homophobic"). They need to study Jewish influence in our foreign policy: the way the Jews lobbied to get us into the two fratricidal bloodbaths, in Europe anyway, known as World Wars One and Two, and the way they have gotten us to pour money and arms into Israel and interject ourselves into Middle East affairs and the consequences of that, including the Iraq wars and 9/11. They also need to give attention to the role of Jews in the arts and entertainment and the mass media, where they are so prevalent and influential. What I'm talking about is the study of Jewish power. Kevin MacDonald has done some good writing in these areas. I find it readable, fascinating, and useful. But his writing is buried in the stacks of university libraries, and anyway, his writing isn't readable to the average person.

Also, our side needs to exploit the possibilities of the Internet before this avenue is shut off to us. Already in Europe, racialist websites—really, any website that contains content that Jews don't like—are banned and made illegal. We need to make it possible for people to hear news from a racialist perspective rather than get it from CBS or CNN.

We need to create racialist films. I was talking about this recently with a woman who wants to create a film festival for films with racially positive content. [Among their complaints about Hollywood movies and television, white racialists point out the frequency with which they depict interracial pairings, citing as examples the recent films *Save the Last Dance, O, Black and White, Monster's Ball*, and *The Truth About Charlie.*]

There is also the challenge to provide an alternative to the poison that the Jewish controlled music industry injects into the veins of our young people. The problem has been that, for the most part, skinhead music is all our side has offered our children. That music is the product of people who tend to be very dysfunctional and with only a superficial interest in racialism. From my dealings with skinheads, most of them see racialism as just another vehicle with which to shock people. Skinhead noise blaring out repels far more white people than it attracts, and the people it does attract are the same kind of dysfunctional people as the ones who are producing the music, the very sort of people we really don't need on our side. If you see footage of a skinhead concert, it's a freak show. White people who see all these skinheads shouting and screaming are very likely going to turn away from racialism. We have to clean up our image. Until we do, we are never going to reach white people.

American politicians are terrified by even the thought that they might get associated with the kinds of things I am talking about here. They won't directly address the crucial problems whites face as a people. There are a few of what I would call crypto-racialists around. By that, I mean people who are racialists, but for tactical reasons they go to great lengths to hide that fact. Pat Buchanan is a crypto-racialist. He understands the issue of race, but he doesn't want to be up front about it, so he kind of dances around the issue. But nonetheless, people with any level of discernment pick up what

Buchanan is talking about. I have read all his books [Buchanan's book that is most relevant in this context is *The Death of the West*]. Buchanan is a major figure in American politics, and I think he's done a lot of good.

I can understand Buchanan's reasons for being less than completely candid, but I think some of the crypto-racialists stay under cover because they just can't bear the thought of other people calling them a racist, and I have less patience with them. Some politicians seem to be infected with the herd mentality that sees racialism as the worst kind of evil, so they can't even admit what they truly think to themselves. These sorts of people embrace various conservative causes and adopt racially positive agendas while all the while trying to stay clear of anybody—including, in some cases, themselves—thinking that they might care about white people. For example, they'll say they oppose Third World immigration into this country on economic grounds, because it takes jobs away from Americans. But the fact of the matter is there are strong counter-arguments to that position. The problem of immigration is fundamentally racial and ought to be argued on those terms, and is best argued on those terms, but because politicians can't bring themselves to deal with immigration in racial terms, their public stance on the issue is weak and ineffective.

While I get frustrated with politicians' lack of candor and think sometimes they are overly cautious, I understand their reluctance to be straightforward, because both parties, supported by the media, join together to smear and exclude overt racialists. That happened to David Duke. [Duke won a seat in the Louisiana state legislature and ran a competitive race for governor in that state and was the presidential candidate on a third party ticket in 1988. More recently, he has confronted legal problems over his alleged misuse of donated funds.] By the way, I got a lot out of Duke's book, *My Awakening*. As circumspect as he has been, Patrick Buchanan hasn't avoided being castigated and, in his last presidential campaign, he was effectively smeared and marginalized.

In any case, time may be running out for a political solution because of the demographic problem. Even if we reach large numbers of white people and persuade them to vote along racially positive lines, you'd still have to contend with the block votes of blacks, Hispanics, Jews, and homosexuals. We saw, for example, in Duke's unsuccessful political runs in Louisiana that even though he got the majority of the white votes, he still lost.

Some have talked about a revolutionary solution, building cadres of revolutionaries who at a future date would presumably accomplish something. Biotechnology may hold out some hope that racial problems can be solved. The denigration of anything like that seems invariably to come from Jews and they have been remarkably effective in winning the day on just about every issue, so we may never see biotechnology applied to racial preservation or improvement. It just may be that our civilization will collapse. We will be swamped with non-whites and that will be the end of us. But then again, a hundred years from now all this insanity we're seeing today might be looked on as something that was ludicrous, crazy, a historical anomaly. Western civilization might clean itself up or even spawn something new and better. That would be wonderful.

9   BLACK METAL

Nadine Taylor, a native Texan, is twenty-three and a senior at the University of Texas in Austin. She comes across as personally grounded and positive in outlook.

Since I was a teenager, I have always been into metal, the music. I've always liked the sound of it and everything else. I especially like black metal. Black metal is a segment of the underground, as we call it, where the bands are more obscure and a little more artistic. They have a big heathen and pagan element, and they are concerned with expressing old European ways, like a lot of old Viking ways. There is a pretty strong anti-Judeo-Christian message in black metal.

I really like the idea that the guys in the bands are very big and strong and tall. They look capable. They look like warriors. And whatever band you are talking about, Danzig or whatever, the front man is very outspoken. I am really drawn to that because that means they aren't just passively consuming what they see. They are trying to apply some sort of critical eye to the world. I like seeing men who are actually self-reliant and not kind of wimpy and ready to just cower in front of someone. I think being against homosexuality as they are is good because homosexuality is promoted as this experimental happy thing that we are all supposed to go through.

Also, I like the slant on history and cultural traditions in the music. Way before I was comfortable with the idea of race, I liked hearing about all these noble and great things that the English or the Germans did. I was very inspired by the idea of greatness, historical greatness, that individuals, actual figures, can rise to greatness, produce art and lead nations and things like that. I appreciate all the emphasis in black metal on responsibility and being noble and courageous and stuff like that.

I was always a pretty quiet girl growing up and I didn't express a lot of things, and so when I saw these guys in bands and that they had a sort of righteous anger, I thought there was really something to that.

It was a good outlet for me. I was finally real grateful to see white kids be very defiant, to stand up for themselves and be very combative. I thought how great that was. White kids don't have much of a place. They don't have things they can turn to. It is starting to be that they are passive and just want do the hip-hop thing. I really liked that a band was standing against that.

When I was about thirteen I started listening to one band, Pantera. They are from Texas, actually. They have managed to become a really big band without MTV or radio airplay. I had a couple of best friends who were sisters. They were a year apart in age. They both got into the aggression of the music. They also thought the lead singer of the band, Philip, was so cool. They thought he was the best looking guy and whatever. I think that is because he was strong and he was good looking, he was. Actually, I met him. I had a big crush on his best friend, and that's how I got to be friends with Phil himself. Both Phil and his friend are very good people. They have their flaws, of course. Like a lot of musicians, they live kind of chaotic lives and have a lot of trouble and whatnot. But they are really good people, warm and affectionate, and, yeah, I liked hanging out with them. This is when I was sixteen and seventeen.

At sixteen I started reading [the late-nineteenth century German philosopher Friedrich] Nietzsche, and he became my favorite author and probably still is. Nietzsche has had a very big influence on me—the concept of overcoming, the concept that power and being very aggressive in war and everything is not an evil thing, or if it is an evil thing, then evil is actually of highest value. Nietzsche's book *Thus Spoke Zarathustra* is so neat because every time you go back to it there are more and more layers to it. You can uncover more. I'm still not done figuring out all the things he throws in.

When I was younger, it was the standard American deal of watching a lot of TV. I was really hooked on TV talk shows. The talk shows sent a kind of flippant message about race. Here's this Mexican gal. Her Mexican boyfriend just got her pregnant and isn't it funny and interesting, like the drama that they go through. Then they would show just regular white people acting trashy too. What I took from that was everyone is pretty much going through the same struggle. At that time, it wasn't occurring to me that there might be constitutional traits and things that differentiate people a lot. I was thinking, how can we be different when we are all going through the drama of love and all this back-and-forth relationship stuff?

As for my racial consciousness in those years, it would be the deal where at school all the kids who were into metal were white, so there was that. I was feeling all these great things from the music, but if someone had turned around and said, "Are you a racist?" I would have said, "Oh, no!" But it's true I had a disdain for rap, and when they tried to mix rock and metal with rap, I thought that was just terrible. I thought that was the most lame thing in the world. And if I was someplace where I didn't know people, like in a mall or something, I would go toward people that looked like me. But basically I was pretty much in line with all the other kids in that I thought anyone who was kind of down on blacks or whatever was just a stodgy old conservative and they're not cool.

Actually, my mom would say stuff to me. She was, like, "I can talk to black people, I can have a civil conversation with them, but I wouldn't want them in my house and I wouldn't want to be friends with them and I certainly wouldn't want to date one," and I remember I would just berate her for that. I thought she was closed-minded and whatnot.

But really I was fairly neutral to whatever—you know, it didn't concern me much. When me and my girlfriend Carrie were sitting around, she confessed to me, "You know, maybe it's not the right thing to say or whatever, but I don't like the Mexican gangs. I don't like the black gangs." I'm like, "Yeah, I hear you." It was no big deal to me.

When I was about eighteen, there was a girl named Casey I was friends with. Casey was a troubled girl. Her mom was an alcoholic—on the wagon and off the wagon—and her dad was in prison for something or another. Casey had gotten into a big fight and was kicked out of her house, and so me and my mom gave her a place to stay kind of the fly, you know. My mom being a normal and very cautious type person, she said, "Casey cannot stay here more than three or four nights, because we can't house a young girl." I said, "I understand." And so I was trying to figure out what this girl Casey was going to do next.

The next day, I went up to a community college—I was taking an extra class there my last year of high school—'cause I had to turn in something. I brought Casey along. We were trying to figure out where she was going to go. She had nowhere to go. I told her, "My mom, who puts a roof over my head, is telling me that you have to have something figured out by tonight."

When we got to the college, Casey started talking to this carload of black guys. Casey was white. She had kind of light brown hair and was a petite girl. She asked these black guys where they thought a motel was. I told Casey, "I'll take you wherever you want to go and drop you off."

Casey had a problem with drugs, which kind of figures in her family, her mom being addicted to alcohol and everything. She made the mistake of putting her drug addiction before any sort of sense, and she decided she wanted to go off with these black guys to try to find some drugs.

At the time I couldn't think of anything objectionable to say about these guys because they were dressed sharp and I felt so constricted because, Lord knows, I didn't want to be branded as a racist. I didn't want to say anything negative against these guys, so I said, "Well, I don't know them from a hole in the wall, I just don't know." And Casey went off with these black guys.

A long story short, Casey got raped by one of the guys in the car. It took her a whole another year to deal with the court and everything. I helped her out being a witness telling what I remembered. It never went to trial. It was a bad deal.

From that experience, it wasn't that I learned that all blacks are bad. What I learned is that this culture and the media and everything inhibit your instincts and your common sense to where you don't want to say, "No Casey, going off with a carload of black guys is not a good idea." It gets you to where you are inhibited from even saying that.

About this same time, I was going to online discussion groups to see what black metal bands people were talking about. I was just there to get information on bands, but I got drawn into what a couple of people who were into black metal had to say against the one world-one race project they said was going on. I would read arguments that said how the Jews have an interest in promoting everyone to kind of melt together. At first that grated on me because, well, I wasn't used to seeing the word Jew used at all, really. I had seen *Schindler's List* and everything, so when I read the word "Jew," I thought, "Oh man, this guy is coming from left field. I can't believe that he is saying this, because this means that he is anti-Semitic." It took a while for me to get past that. But I could tell this guy was really well read for one thing, and he was really educated in philosophy. I was impressed with that. Then I started thinking there's a reason that these black metal bands are celebrating a heathen or pagan tradition and why they often rail against the Jews and have such aggression and talk warlike.

I never found out who this guy was that was posting exactly, but he would get into these ideological arguments and he would just basically argue all the leftists and multicultural-type people totally into the ground. At the end of each of his little posts, he would have a link to both the National Alliance and the World Church of the Creator, and one other organization I think. At first, I was a little skeptical. I thought, "Well, he seems to mention the Jews a lot," and I thought maybe he is just some sort of reactionary person that I shouldn't be listening to. But the more I listened to him, he was so reasoned and thought out that probably the eightieth time I saw his name up there, I finally followed a link to the National Alliance and that's when I got more interested in racial concerns. I think the National Alliance was the first of the three links that he always included, so I went to that web site first.

I wasn't immediately struck with the notion that I needed to be a member of the National Alliance, but it got me to where I would visit the site and I started to know who Dr. [William] Pierce was. So then when on different places on the Internet people would post articles or broadcasts that Dr Pierce had written or quotes that he had said, there was that name recognition and I thought, "Oh, that's that guy." I was still a little cautious, though, 'cause I wasn't used to the idea of being associated with anything that people would call right wing and stuff. But more and more I would read the things that Dr. Pierce said and I thought they made a heck of a lot of sense.

Then eventually I was corresponding online with a guy from Detroit. He was into a lot of the music and everything I was, and he was a racial guy as well, even more so than I would have claimed to be at the time. In our e-mails back and forth, one day I said, "I may look into this group called the National Alliance because I think they have a unit around where I live and I want to see what they are about." He e-mailed me back and said, "That's funny you mention that because I'm a member myself." So this Internet friend I had could pretty much vouch that the National Alliance was a good organization and very sharp-minded and all that. So from that I decided, well, then yeah, I'll definitely check it out.

So I went to a local National Alliance unit meeting here. I was really impressed with the people. That's really what did it for me. The ideas, I knew I agreed with most everything. I was going to try to check out the people and I was really impressed with them. A lot of white women, when they think of anything racial like the Alliance that says be proud of your race, be proud of who you are, immediately think of skinheads, just getting drunk and "sieg heiling," and that has a lot to do with the movies they have been watching and everything else. And maybe they have been programmed to think that strong white men are brutish and evil and they just need a soft sensitive wimp or something like that. So they never get to meet the kind of people I met. I joined after the first meeting. It just took me a while to get my paperwork in and whatnot.

My first year at college at the University of Texas, I remember walking through the main mall area and there were always different groups protesting the mistreatment of somebody or another. And there was the black coalition of engineers and the Pakistani young nurses association and all that. I remember thinking that there is nothing for just regular white people and so I felt pretty alienated. I looked at all these little booths and I didn't want to get involved with any of it. I didn't see anything that appealed to me. The only group that was mostly white kids was the university skeptics society and I just thought they were a bunch of cynical losers, basically, and I didn't like their vibe. So I was pretty turned off by the whole deal. What I got from that was that other races were exalted, but if you are white there is not that actual place for you.

The past couple of years, I have come to know the German poet, Friedrich Hölderlin. He wrote in the 1800s and Nietzsche was influenced by him. I took a graduate class last year and I wrote a term paper showing that Hölderlin was a nationalist but his nationalism was rooted in the folk, the *volk*. He didn't touch upon the political in his work. It was always very connected to the earth and ancient traditions and the communal spirit. I'm glad I came across Hölderlin. He's a pretty great poet.

In a literature class last semester, the professor had us read a book by Ronald Wright called *Stolen Continents: The Americas Through Indian Eyes Since 1492*. It was about how the avaricious white man had plundered and pillaged and was hell-bent on killing everyone and getting rich—that was the orientation all whites had coming to the New World. I remember there was one statement in the book that the achievements of the Europeans were technological and not social. I felt that deep down the professor knew, as I did, how ridiculous that statement was and how much of a hatred toward Western civilization that kind of statement promoted, but he didn't criticize it. It made me frustrated. I was sitting there in class and I just looked down in my notebook and started doodling. I was pretty disappointed.

The professor had us write an essay and I basically said that the book was painting whites as evil and that the author had added all sorts of nasty things and I could tell it was personal for him. I got an A on the paper. The next essay I wrote for that course was on the Founding Fathers. I said I thought that Jefferson and Hamilton when they were laying the groundwork for everything, that they may not have anticipated the peculiar racial admixture that would be in the country later. When I turned that paper in the professor wrote on it in red letters, "See me." And I was, like, "Oh boy."

So I went to his office, and he just asked me what I meant by the peculiar admixtures of cultures and races. I said that with increasing pluralism comes increasing problems, and then I mentioned how first northern Europeans had immigrated to the New World, and then after that African slaves were freed, and then southern Europeans came, and now, these days, there are immigrants from Asia and Mexico. But I said it in such a civil manner that he said, "OK, I was just trying to…"—well, actually he didn't say anything; he just let me out and gave me an A.

Even though he didn't really challenge me, I took him calling me into the office to mean that you maybe are skating on thin ice, so to speak. I felt he was kind of trying to put the brakes on what he felt might be going in too extreme a direction. When he saw the second essay and I still was bringing up a racial thing that could be construed as pro-white, I think he was trying to tell me there is a certain point I shouldn't go past or there are certain things I shouldn't say. I thought that was a possibility of what he was trying to do. It was a little ambiguous.

This incident was different for me than it would have been two years ago. Now, with me being more aware of things and more secure in what I believe, when I followed him to his office, I was pretty calm. I sat in his office and kind of adopted my super friendly exterior. I asked him what classes he was teaching next semester and everything. When I was sitting there, I did feel grilled, but I had expected it, which for me is very helpful in being able to calm myself down.

I would definitely call myself a white nationalist now. I want to preserve my race and my heritage. I think it is important to follow nature's dictums, and that means staying within my own race. I believe the white race has done the most impressive world historical things and that we shouldn't dilute ourselves biologically or culturally. Basically, to me, "us" is white people in the United States, but I think of the white people in Europe fighting for the cause as us too. I really like the idea of actually sacrificing for my people. The notion of sacrifice is very noble. People are just these little atoms and don't have a concept of anything higher or greater than their own individual lives. I don't want to live like that.

I go to [National] Alliance meetings once a month. The unit coordinator and his wife have become like my best friends. Goodness, it helps to find good people. They are probably a couple of the best people I have ever met. Really, what has happened to me is that I have been so busy meeting neat people in the white power movement and in white nationalism, whether it is the Alliance or kids on the street who listen to resistance music, that I'm so busy with that why would I even want to hang out with people outside my race?

My dad has some land in Oklahoma. I've noticed that when I go out to there now, I'm a lot more interested than I used to be just hearing about what good white folks have to say. When I was in high school, I could never be bothered with that. So I think I've become a lot more able to connect with people, feel good will toward people. Before, I might have said, "Oh gosh, there's some young rural couple with twenty kids!" or whatever, and, "Oh, isn't that terrible, that's so unsophisticated!" Now I look at it and I'm like, "Wow, that's great!" I admire the discipline and what it takes to be able to raise your kids and to have a lot of kids, 'cause they are pretty neat.

I'd like to help white people recover the arts in a sense. When I go around my school and look at who's in the art department, it's all these, like, really frail, pasty, gay people, gay guys, and it's these very leftist and communist-type people. A lot of postmodernism, whether it is in the art world or literary criticism, I think is so harmful. It keeps breaking down white people's consciousness, but it is looked at as cool. I want to help develop something that is cool for white kids. I help out with Resistance, both the magazine and the web site [www.resistance.com]. I wrote a couple reviews of CDs for the magazine. With my interest in music, I think it is real important for the young kids who are real vulnerable these days to have there be a very cool, a very sharp, look, like a style? Because, you know, these rap kids have their ridiculous style and the baggy pants and everything. I'd like to help show and popularize that being a strong healthy white person is really a beautiful and cool thing, 'cause kids really want to go off on what's cool.

I definitely would like a family. I don't want one quite yet, though, even though a real close friend of mine has done a great job of having a family pretty early. She is just a year older than I am and has a little boy and a little girl. One of the things I find out about a guy now is if he eventually wants a family. A future husband will definitely have to share my racial views. Right now, what I'm going to do in terms of a job and things like that, I'm pretty confused. I've taken a big interest in photography and the visual arts. I don't know whether I want to do something artistic or go to graduate school in literature or psychology. But I feel as if I have come a long way personally and in overcoming personal obstacles and, on a larger scale, just finding the right way to look at things that helps me have a good outlook on life and contribute to something that will outlast me.

10   I WAS WILLING TO DIE

Eric Owens is thirty-two and lives in the Los Angeles area. He is married with no children and works in the building trades. He has a formidable physical presence and direct manner.

I have always been politically conscious. My parents split up when I was one and I was raised by a leftist father in northern California until I was five and then we moved to Los Angeles. My father remarried when I was in elementary school. When I was a little kid, I had pictures of Marx and Mao and a Viet Cong flag on my wall. I remember doing stuff for Cesar Chavez and the farm workers. When I got old enough to think for myself, I rejected communism. I thought it was totalitarian. But really that didn't bother me as much as the fact that it was dishonest. I had been around communists enough to know they were always scheming and lying. I was sympathetic to anarchism some, but I never really became an anarchist. Pacifism is what attracted me. When I was thirteen years old, I was going to anti-nuclear marches and stuff like that. At those kinds of gatherings, I would encounter communists who would pose as anarchists. I actually got conned into going to a couple of communist rallies because they billed them as anarchist or pacifist rallies, and those people were neither anarchists nor pacifists.

When I was in junior high school, I realized that pacifism in practice just doesn't work on a personal level. I wasn't the biggest guy on the block, so people found me an easy target. They would pick fights with me and I'd actually be trying to talk to them while they were punching me in the face. I found that when I started beating the crap out of people who were doing that sort of thing, peace was instantly restored. Ironically, a couple of fistfights gave me a peaceful life that I could never have attained through pacifism. So I started asking myself, if pacifism doesn't work on a personal level, how can I be sure it will work on a larger level?

I have always been really musically inclined. My father liked music and played it. I have been a musician since I was old enough to pick up an instrument. I moved from one instrument to another—guitar, flute, piano, accordion, bagpipes. I play a lot of instruments. I never liked mindless music. I liked music that had to do with politics or social issues. I got involved with anarcho-pacifist punk music. There were bands from England. We're talking about the early- to mid-'80s. A collective called Crass was really big. Then Oi! music started coming around—bands like 4Skins and Blitz. These were skinhead bands, basically, that were preaching a working class and patriotic and violent ethos, a very street-smart message.

I thought, yeah, you know, instead of looking like a slob like the punk rockers, it is better to be clean-cut and have some self-respect and hold your head up. The music was saying you have worth, your country has worth, your ancestors have worth, and you should take pride in yourself. And you have certain responsibilities. They were very low-level responsibilities, just be a proud worker and work hard and be honest and forthright and patriotic. For a white young person going to school where the teachers are telling you that you're worthless and your country's worthless and your forefathers are worthless and you've got something to be ashamed of, and you have people harassing you at the same time, it was a message that really resonated with me and a couple of my friends.

As time went along, my racial views developed. I listened to racial bands from England like Screwdriver and Brutal Attack and I agreed with their message and I identified with it. Even if I didn't agree with the more extreme aspects of it, I agreed with the general feeling of what they were getting across. At that time I thought, you know, hey, there's nice black people and there's nice everybody, so you can't paint everyone with the same brush and all that. Screwdriver was affiliated with the National Front party in England, so I started to read *The Bulldog*, a publication the National Front puts out for young people. Me and my friends started to contact racial groups in the United States and I read books I found out about through them. A couple of them were *The Turner Diaries* [by Andrew Macdonald (William Pierce)] and *White Power* by George Lincoln Rockwell.

I also went to my high school library and read *Mein Kampf* cover to cover. That really opened doors for me racially. It explained a lot of things that just hadn't made sense to me. Like, if blacks are equal to us—and I believed that they were, because I was told that they were by everyone, there was no disputing it—I certainly was curious about why, no matter how much you gave them, they could never measure up. And they sure didn't seem very intelligent, and even though many of them had better lives financially and socially than me and many of my white friends had, why do we still seem to be more intelligent than they are? I read *Mein Kampf* and saw that actually the case wasn't closed, that there were people advocating racial differences, and that those views made a lot more sense than the racial story that I was hearing in school and everywhere else. I got Hitler's side of the story, like about Hitler's supposed dastardly strategy of the "big lie." I thought, hey, either these people telling me what's gone on don't know what they are talking about or they have been lying to me.

I got into reading about Nazism. In a *Time-Life* book, there was a poster from World War II. It had a brutish looking guy and underneath his picture was *untermensch*—subhuman. The *Time-Life* book said this was propaganda teaching that Russian soldiers were less than human. Then I went to the Simon Wiesenthal Center. [The Simon Wiesenthal Center, headquartered in Los Angeles, is a Jewish organization whose stated purpose is preserving the memory of the Holocaust and combating anti-Semitism.] There I saw the exact same poster and it said it was propaganda convincing Germans that the mentally ill and handicapped were subhuman and should be put to death. I thought, OK, here's two official sources who have completely different views about what the very same poster was for, and I thought either they don't know what they are talking about and this isn't real history or they are lying. This got to be a pattern: the more I went to the source, the more I saw discrepancies.

I became a skinhead in high school. That phase of my life lasted a long time, into my early twenties. It was a folk scene, basically. I had never been much attracted to mainstream rock music because it just didn't seem to have anything to do with me. Here was some guy up on the stage prancing around like he's a god and you're a loyal fan.

I had never been into that. In punk, the musicians and the fans were the same. Punk bands were like-minded people who started bands for their views or for fun or for whatever, but it least it wasn't profit-motivated. And the same was true for skinheads. The skinhead groups were skinheads themselves who started their own groups and there was no separation between the musician and the listener. They were a community, really. I got caught up in the skinhead scene. I believed what they believed and so I started to outwardly project the image that I saw and admired.

By the time I graduated from high school, me and a couple of my friends were basically covered with tattoos. You're trying to prove to your comrades that you're in this for the long haul. You are dedicated and this isn't just something you are doing for a week or two. You are in this for life. And you want to show some people that you're someone they shouldn't mess with. When you are an adolescent going to high school—I went to a predominately black high school, I might add—you want to be seen as a formidable foe if that needs to be. I never got anything on my hands or above my neck, so I was able to wear long sleeve shirts at work and look clean-cut. At school I didn't care what people thought.

Skinheads started in England in the late 1960s, but people in the United States in the mid-'80s didn't know what they were. If you told people here you were a skinhead, you'd have to explain it. There were only a few skinheads in the whole country and we all knew each other. Skinheads here in Los Angeles would know if there was one lone skinhead in Nevada or New York. We'd all write to each other. People thought we were ROTC guys from high school or something, but then the Nazi/KKK/skinhead image started going out on the talk shows and things changed on a dime. All of a sudden the blacks at school knew who they were dealing with. Most of them didn't harass me because they had known me for so many years, but of course there were always new people at the school, so I did get in a fair number of fights over it. Although there was violence at that school all the time anyway—gang fights, shootings, you name it. Fighting was normal there. I got in fights over all sorts of issues. There were racial fights, but there were also other fights, lots of fights.

A real turning point in me becoming a dedicated racialist was when I was eighteen. There was a racial concert, the first one of its kind, called Aryan Woodstock up in Napa Valley in northern California. Me and a bunch of my friends who at the time were sympathetic but not racial per se drove up there because, more than anything, we were music fans. We had been reading a lot of racial publications, but we thought a lot of it was probably overblown. You know, they'd say we don't have freedom of speech, and we thought, well, sure we do.

When we got up there, the police made us walk for miles through the hills. It was clear to us they were doing everything they could to stop our right to speech and assembly and to harass us so we would either leave or never want to do it again. A lot of communists and homosexual groups and the Jewish Defense League were there attacking people and the police didn't lift a finger to help the people being attacked. The Jewish Defense League actually beat on a ninety-six-year-old war veteran. And they beat up a thirteen-year-old kid. Forty-five-year-old men pummeled a child young enough to be their own son. I realized these were not men like my father. I could never imagine my father and a group of his friends stomping a thirteen-year-old boy. I was just infuriated.

I saw the conflict between Jews and regular Americans right in front of me. I saw them try to stop me from even having the right to hear an opposing view, and I saw the police colluding with them, and I saw them attacking people. I thought about when I had gone to black power reggae concerts where they were openly and militantly pro-black and praising [Louis] Farrakhan and slandering white people. It had been building for a long time, but it all came together at that concert. These people are on one side and I'm on another. I realized that it isn't about whether you meet a nice Jewish or black person at the bus stop one day and they smile at you. This is about our survival and our way of life. Right then, I decided that I was going to dedicate my life to creating a healthy and peaceful white society. I still have pacifist motivations deep down, but as odd as it might sound, that hasn't stopped me from being revolutionary and pro-violent. What I want in the end is peace, but sometimes the only way to achieve peace is to stand up and fight for your personal space.

Up to the time of that concert, I had called myself a patriot. Now I was a racist. That meant to me that there was no more time to waste and that I had a job to do, and it was to make a homeland for white people so that we could have a place to live and celebrate our own identity without rival groups infringing on our rights or competing with us on our own land. If that could happen here in the United States, that was fine, and if it had to happen somewhere else, that was fine too, but it had to happen. Whether it was in Europe or on this continent, the whole continent or one state, I didn't know. I just knew it had to happen and that I was going to help create it and I would move to wherever I was needed. I decided that I wasn't going to be a bystander in the struggle.

The commitment I made at that Aryan Woodstock concert fourteen years ago has never changed and never will change. From then on, I knew where I stood. I have been a serious activist since that time. Actually, I was an activist before that, too. I have always felt that the world doesn't have to be the way it is, that you can always make things better, that no matter how good things may be, they can always improve, and so you have to be involved in life. I have always wanted a peaceful society where I could raise a family and have a small home and just be content. Nuclear war and nuclear accidents do not lend themselves to that life, so as a child I took the obvious step of participating in anti-nuclear activities. As more and more of the world's problems became evident to me and what was actually causing them, I just shifted the direction in which I was firing, but I have always been firing.

I was in an Oi! band at the time—which is another name for a skinhead band—and as soon as I got home after the Aryan Woodstock concert, I talked with the other members of the band about whether we should be an overtly racial band or just stick to the patriotic songs we have been playing. The key members of the band agreed with me that we should become a racial band and that if the other guys didn't like it they were free to leave, and that's what happened. We recorded a couple of albums in Germany.

In 1990, I stopped playing rock music and sold all my electric instruments and decided to only play acoustic music. I stayed racial, but I decided that rock music didn't hold anything for me anymore. I found it hollow, just very stupid and shallow and juvenile, and the more I read and understood about the world, I couldn't any longer simplify things to just basic slogans and basic beats. Rock had nothing of beauty in it and I wanted to make the world a more beautiful place, not a more ugly and minimalistic and brutal place. I got sick of the lunkhead mentality that went along with rock music. I also wanted to get back into my roots. I had been raised on Irish music and I'm Irish myself. My father was very much into Irish music and played it. I wanted to play the music of my heritage and not the music of the commercial multi-racial system which I felt rock to be. I thought rock music was degenerate, non-white music.

For me, it was a matter of identity, a matter of who I am. I wanted to take part in the traditions of Ireland for the same reason I couldn't stand to sit in a high school class and hear a teacher denigrate the people who built this country. Even though many of the Irish bands were leftist and the music wasn't really racial, it was still hundreds of years old and traditional, and it was my heritage no matter who was singing or what they were singing about. I always loved Irish music and I always loved the dancing. They were things of beauty, and in Los Angeles there is not much beauty of any kind. Although I should point out that it wasn't just traditional Irish music I liked. I have always been a fan of traditional American music as well. Like I have always been a fan of Doc Watson and American flatpickers.

There's a very strong nationalist message in Irish music. When people are struggling for independence, they pick up on their traditional roots and magnify nationalist themes. With my dad being a leftist of Irish decent, there was IRA music in my house all the time. This was during a time when things were really tense in Northern Ireland: Bobby Sands, the hunger strike in H-Block, and all that stuff was going on. [In 1981, Sands and nine other IRA members starved themselves to death protesting prison conditions.]

I started playing Irish music and then I put my own racial ballads in there. Then I started developing a liking for other types of European folk music as well, and so I put Scottish and Welsh tunes and other things into the mix. Now, I consider myself a Celtic folk musician. I have recorded a couple of folk albums that have a militant pro-white message. I have played in some coffee houses in

LA. I used to play the Aryan Fests, basically outdoor skinhead concerts, but I found that I wasn't reaching people in the way that I wanted to. I had hoped that I could imbue people with a deeper sense of their race and their traditions, but I found that I was just providing music for people to drink alcohol to and so I basically stopped playing in those places. I felt like I was wasting my time. Now, just about the only time I play is if a group such as the National Alliance is having a gathering. Those are people who can understand what I am trying to do.

Letting go of the skinhead persona started when the music changed. It was time for me to move on, but I still felt a lot of loyalty to it. It had done a lot for me as far as giving me a strong white identity when I was young. The skinhead movement is better than the media portrays it as being, but it isn't as good as it needs to be. The skinhead identity could be a stepping-stone towards creating a really productive white individual, but instead it puts window dressing on dysfunctional cosmopolitan white youth and doesn't go any further than that. It advocates marring your body. It advocates what is brutish and primitive. It advocates alcoholism to the extreme. It advocates prison instead of college. It advocates the working class as opposed to becoming the ruling class. When I see all of the young kids dropping out of school and tattooing their arms like they are Tahitian villagers, and getting themselves thrown in prison for a fistfight with a nigger instead of going to college and becoming a hundred thousand dollar a year attorney who could win us court battles and help fund media to reach our people, I'm really disappointed. The racial leaders who have capitalized on the skinhead movement have failed our youth by not steering them in the right direction. By glorifying the thuggishness of this identity they are leading these kids into a life of alcoholism, street violence, prison, and a dead-end jobs.

We need educated people in the white nationalist movement— attorneys and doctors and engineers. The downside of not producing or attracting these kinds of people is that there are too few in the legal system to defend our rights and defend our organizations from being sacked by people like the Southern Poverty Law Center. [The SPLC has been successful in a number of civil suits against white racialist organizations and individuals.] And it means there has been too little funding for alternative media, so we have not been able to reach people with our message as effectively as we might. And skinheads don't become revolutionary cadre either. If you are looking for the militant revolutionaries, people who will lay it all out on the line and create violence in the street, it hasn't been skinheads. Richard Baumhammer wasn't a skinhead. He was an attorney who graduated at the top of his class. Buford Furrow was an engineer. Benjamin Smith had a long history of excellent scholastic achievement up to his episode. If we go back further than that, we have Robert Jay Mathews, who was not a hooligan or a rock fan or a drunk. He was a family man. Kathy Ainsworth was a schoolteacher. Sam Bowers was a USC graduate. [In May of 2000, Richard Baumhammer, thirty-four, went on a shooting and blaze-setting spree in southwestern Pennsylvania targeting Jews and immigrants, leaving five dead and a sixth clinging to life. In August of 1999 in Los Angeles, Buford Furrow Jr., thirty-eight, killed a Hispanic postal worker and wounded five at a Jewish community center. In July of 1999, Benjamin Smith, twenty-one, went on a shooting rampage in Illinois and Indiana targeting blacks, Jews, and Asians, killing two and wounding nine before killing himself. Robert Mathews formed an insurrectionary white separatist group called The Order in 1983 and was killed a year later near Seattle, Washington in a shootout with the FBI. With her husband, Kathy Ainsworth bombed a Jackson, Mississippi synagogue in 1967. She was killed by a hail of FBI bullets in June of 1968 as she attempted to place a bomb on the front porch of the home of an Anti-Defamation League leader. Sam Bowers, the Imperial Wizard of the White Knights of the Ku Klux Klan of Mississippi, was found guilty of authorizing the 1964 murder of Michael Schwerner, the head of the Congress of Racial Equality office in Meridian, Mississippi.]

I went to a community college and then a university in southern California, graduating with a major in French and Italian literature. In the beginning, I precipitated in some extremely heated racial discussions, and one time a fistfight broke out in the class. People weren't used to hearing the opinions I expressed in an open forum and some of the blacks went ballistic and punched whites in the class because they had agreed with me. A friend of mine who was also racial wrote a paper saying the Holocaust was overblown and the Jewish professor told him to leave the class. My degree was important to me, and I realized that starting fights and antagonizing Jewish professors who held the key to my future wasn't the way to get it. So I became a "low-profiler" in college. And anyway, by the time I got to the university level there were very few blacks because they couldn't keep up, so when I got into a higher level of education I no longer had to deal with them.

Another key turning point for me was after college, just a couple of years ago, happened when I was traveling in Europe. My record company was throwing a concert in Sweden and I went just because I had nothing better to do. The concert was raided by the police and a riot ensued and the police tear-gassed us and beat up a lot of people. The long and short of it is that me and the other Americans got locked up in solitary confinement and I was angered by it and so I refused to eat or drink. I figured that maybe if I die in a cell it would incite white youth to be more militant, to be angry and to fight harder. On the fifth day of my hunger strike, they let me out of jail. They kept everyone else for over a month. I couldn't hold down any solid food for several days after I got out and it felt like Mike Tyson was pounding on my kidneys.

Looking back on it, what I did was pointless, but it did have one important outcome for me: I realized I was willing to die. I had always thought that the reason there had been no revolution must be that the leaders in the movement are afraid to make the sacrifices that leading their people into a revolution would require. When I found out that I could freely of myself give up my life, I thought, well, then why not me as a leader, maybe I should be the one to do it.

So when I got back to California I started a racial group called the Aryan International Movement. The idea was that it would have a more militant leaning and be more socially active than the other groups that were around and that it would move things forward quicker. I saw it as the precursor to a Hamas-type organization in America. [Hamas—a word meaning courage and bravery—is a radical and often violent Islamic organization whose goal is an Islamic Palestine "from the Mediterranean Sea to the Jordan River."] I envisioned it eventually becoming an all-encompassing organization that would involve itself in schooling and social services, and that it would engage in militant combat. About a hundred people joined up within a few months.

A year into it, I realized that I was not going to achieve what I had set out to achieve through this organization. People's commitment just wasn't there. I could fill a room, no problem, but I couldn't get anybody to do anything. After beating my head against the wall for a year trying to motivate people, I realized that the National Alliance is the group that is doing the most good with their long-term, slow-growth approach. I realized you can only move as fast as you've got support to move. The Alliance is accomplishing what can be accomplished in the current circumstance better than I can, so I decided that rather than start another group it would be better for me to become a member of the Alliance. And that is what I have done. I don't go to unit meetings, though. I've always felt that it is a waste of time to sit around and argue with people about what's the best thing to do. If you want help with something, I'll be glad to help you or do what I think best, but I don't want to sit around and argue.

When I tried to run my own group, I realized how important money is. I saw how futile it is to try to run a group composed of a membership unable to fund the group's projects. So I try to be the kind of member of the Alliance I would have liked in my own organization. Besides my dues, I give as much extra money as I can, and right now I'm trying to build myself up career-wise so that I can give not a hundred dollars at a time but several thousand dollars at a time.

11   SAFE IN MAINE

Carolyn Davies* is fifty-three and a widow and lives in Massachusetts after spending most of her life in Texas. She works for the government in the area of social services.

My first awareness that there were different races came when I was a little girl, about five or six. This was in the mid-1950s. We were living in California. We hadn't moved to the South yet. We visited my mother's relatives in Texas. I went downtown with my mother and my two aunts. We went to a department store and they were talking and shopping and I was just sort of looking around like children do, and I noticed that they had two water fountains on the wall. One of them had a sign that said "colored." I had never seen anything like that before, so I ran up to my mother and said, "Oh mommy, they have colored water over there! Can I have some?" My mother was a very sweet, precious, loving Christian person who didn't have a mean bone in her body. She tried to explain to me what colored people were and why here in Texas colored people had to drink out of different fountains and go to different bathrooms. She was very calm and gentle, but it was just sort of like I had never heard of such a thing. It was just so foreign to me. That moment has stuck with me. It is one of a few memories I have from when I was very young.

My family traveled a lot with my dad's work—all over the country and in Canada—and eventually we moved to Texas when I was in high school. It was a white school, but they had hand-picked about ten exceptional black students from black schools to go there. One of them had good speech and debate talent and those were areas I was interested in, so I got to know him quite well from our various activities. He was a really nice kid. I remember one time when we were coming back from a speech tournament. We dropped him off at his house and it was in a really run-down area of town, and he seemed sort of embarrassed. I thought how difficult it must be for him. It

96

was like he was on display. He had to be perfect. He had to prove to the white people that he was acceptable and like us, and there was his really dilapidated house. I don't know, it just really dug at me somehow, and it has stayed with me ever since.

In the fall of 1967, I went off to a private liberal arts college in Minnesota. When I got there, I was assigned a black roommate, a real sweet girl from Chicago. Looking back on it, I suppose they put me with her thinking something like, "Oh, this poor ignorant person from the South"—me—"we have to save her because she must be a horrible bigot," which I wasn't. I don't think it was just an accident that the one person in the school from the South is the only white person who ended up with a black roommate. She was on a full scholarship and she studied really hard. She was very cliquish with the other dozen or so black students on campus. Sometimes they would come to our room and that was fine with me, it was her room, too. I realized how difficult it was for the black students. They were on trial. They had to succeed. They couldn't miss a class. They had to make good grades.

The college I went to had very high academic standards. Probably most students who went there were in the top ten percent of their high school class. The black students may have been the top students in their high schools, but I don't think they were on the same level as the white students. So they had to work really hard to prove that they could keep up with the rest of us. My roommate was under so much pressure, even from the other black students. I remember them calling her an "oreo" a couple of times and that really hurt her. I just think it was very hard for her.

When I got out into the world, I became a social worker. I had grown up in a family with a lot of advantages. Not so much financially—we did okay, we were comfortable, but we weren't wealthy or anything—but we had background and breeding. We had a great deal of pride in our family history, our British heritage. I was taught that as a Christian I should have a Christ-like serving nature. I wanted to do for others who didn't have the benefits I did. As a social worker, I worked for a number of years with all types of people—abused children, senior citizens in nursing homes, severely handicapped and developmentally disabled people, and mentally ill in a children's psychiatric hospital. This was in Texas. I had moved back there.

My clients were from all different backgrounds: black and Hispanic and lower class white. Frankly, over time I started to become disillusioned with them. I saw that they had different desires and different ways than what I had expected and hoped. A lot of them, I came to realize, didn't really want to solve their problems and really didn't have much of any impulse to do anything to better themselves. More than anything, they just wanted someone to do things for them and take care of them so they didn't have to have any responsibility for their lives. I saw that the basic caliber of people really differs, that it isn't just that some have situations that hold them back and keep them down. Like everybody else, I had been brainwashed in college to think that everybody is basically equal. Your parents mortgage the farm to send you off to college to learn from these people, and so you assume the professors know what they are talking about and that they are telling you the truth, which I eventually found out they weren't.

When I was growing up, there were people who were from abused homes. There were people whose parents were alcoholics. There were people whose fathers or mothers had abandoned them. But they had exposure in school and in church and with their friends to what a normal life is like. That gave them the opportunity to see, "I don't have to stay in this kind of a life, I can do better." Years ago, people wanted to try to do better, and parents—no matter how poor they were, no matter how bad their situation was—worked hard to give their children something a little bit better than what they had.

So many of the parents I worked with seemed perfectly happy for their children to stay in the horrible situations they were in. We have fourth and fifth generation welfare families now. We have parents who don't care if their children do even worse in life than they did. That, to me, is the problem. And I think that there's a lot of racial and ethnic influence in that. Whites are taking on the standards of minorities. I don't think that is exclusively what is going on—the way the welfare system operates contributes to the problem—but I do believe it is a big factor. Although, for that matter, to a big extent the current welfare system is an accommodation to black and Hispanic approaches to life, so there is a racial dimension there too.

In Texas, where I lived until recently when I moved to Massachusetts, I had a lot of experience working with Hispanics and blacks. Particularly with black people, in their philosophy or value system, being a jerk is great. You know, being rude and crude and foul-mouthed and putting people down and being irresponsible, the way you see it in the black recording artists and the athletic stars now—that's what I mean. Blacks take pride in being that way. There's something admirable about it to them. It's like they no longer have to meet our standards, white standards. They can do whatever they want and if we don't like it, there's something wrong with us.

I'm going to sound like I am a hundred I know, but when I was growing up, people had manners. Everyone was expected to behave in a certain way. People who didn't were looked down upon or ostracized. It wasn't acceptable to be crude or rude or obnoxious or foul-mouthed. I think it started with Muhammad Ali. At least that's the first person I can ever remember behaving like that, like so many kids especially act today, and I'm talking about white kids. Ali was a very bright young black man who had a tremendous physical talent in his boxing, but he was also a smart-mouthed jackass. We accepted that and even loved him for it and thought it was fabulous that he did that. There were black celebrities at that time like [singers] Lena Horne and Leslie Uggams, and you had Arthur Ashe in tennis, for example. They were all very much ladies and gentlemen. But Muhammad Ali came around and made it cool to be smart-mouthed and smart-alecky.

So I do see the influence of race and different value systems helping to diminish our culture and our country. I'll give you another example of the kind of thing I am talking about. The apartment complex where I was living had been all white, but then the composition started changing. Some new neighbors moved in next to me who were from Mexico. I'd say "Good morning" and "How are you?" and they would just smile and say "Thank you"—they didn't speak much English. They had almost no furniture. It was a family of a husband and wife and three kids, but there were ten or twelve other Mexican people over there all the time. They would all go out and sit out on the stairs and drink Cokes and eat candy and throw trash and garbage all over the place. When I tried to get in and out, I could barely do it because they were sitting there. The kids would stare in my windows. Their daughter and her boyfriend would hang out in their apartment when she got off school and they would scream and have fights and curse at each other. Many times, they would do it right outside my window. One time, I thought the young lady might be being abused or something and I asked her if she was all right, did she want me to call the police or her parents. "No!" she shouted at me and started back screaming obscenities at her boyfriend.

Black people also started moving into the apartment complex and it started getting to where they would come through at two or three in the morning with their car stereos blasting and having wild parties and things like that. Yelling and screaming and swearing and carrying on was normal for them. And I guess they have a right to live that way, but I don't want them underneath me or next door to me. I got tired of listening to it and picking up trash. I just don't want to live like that. I started to think that if I wanted a decent life I would have to run away from these people. And why should I have to do that? Why can't they live up to my standards instead of me having to leave in order to get away from their standards?

I remember saying to a friend one time, "I just can't stand being around black people who are so crude and vulgar and foul-mouthed and overbearing and obnoxious." Before she could get on her high horse and say, "How dare you say such a thing?" I said, "But I don't like white people who are like that either." So for me it is not so much the race or the ethnicity, it's the behavior. I don't like being around vulgar, low-class people, period. I like being around upper class people or nice, normal, decent middle class people.

I was making a fairly good living and was able to move from the apartment complex I was in, but there are a lot of Anglo people who aren't as fortunate as I am and they are still back there living with all that. For example, there were some neighbors who were just lovely people, an elderly couple. She was in her seventies and he was in his eighties and he was very ill. They were really not physically able to move and, secondly, it is very expensive and where would they go? I tried to help them out, but I just wasn't able to do enough. They were trapped there, so they have to put up with what is going on. It is just awful for them because they had no options.

Back in the early 1990s, I did some volunteer work at a bookstore. It had a lot of things about our founding fathers, what their goals and desires were, the kind of country they wanted to make, and so on, and I spent a lot of time reading those books. I began to be very proud of what they had done and in the fact that my ancestors were part of that. I began to get an even greater pride in my European heritage. Someone in my family did extensive genealogy and found out that one of my ancestors was the first civilian ever knighted in England back in the 1300s. He had saved the life of King Richard during the peasants' revolt and he was Lord Mayor of London twice. That was so exciting for me to discover. I was just so proud of the people from whom I came and my heritage that, even though that was hundreds of years ago, I felt like it was still in my genes somehow. As my relative delved more deeply, I found out that my family on both sides had been very active in the colonial movement in this country. One of my ancestors had been governor of one of the colonies and things like that. So I began to have a tremendous pride in who I was and where I had come from. I was probably around forty at that point.

I am very patriotic and love America and have great respect for the Founding Fathers, who felt that they had a great gift from God. I think our country was founded on wonderful principles. But now our country's founders are being portrayed as monsters instead of being revered for the abilities and knowledge and courage and strength they had. I believe America was intended to be a white European country. That doesn't mean we don't want anyone here from other races. I don't want to go back to exclusion and segregation. But I do want people here who love this country and are proud of it, and who want to be Americans and who don't constantly put this country down and tell us how horrible everybody was and how horrible everybody is now.

I read a lot of things I got from this bookstore about the Frankfurt School kind of theory that is trying to change this country. The Frankfurt School was a group of Jewish scholars in Germany during Hitler's time and they fled to America. Their ideas are the root of what we call political correctness. The Frankfurt School intellectuals are the ones who started all this about racism and sexism and homophobia and, you know, it's not acceptable to be proud of who you are if you're white and it's not acceptable to feel critical of any groups that do not behave like normal people. I became conscious that what is going on in society isn't just an accident. Somebody is trying to change America. They are trying to bring about what they would call a utopian world, and that involves destroying the white race, or compromising it, weakening it, taking away its power, its place in things, you know?

I don't believe the leaders of the politically correct movements have any real desire to help anyone—the civil rights movement, the various homosexual rights movements, and the women's movement. By the way, what a crock feminism is. Where did all the men go? I think the people at the top of those movements are doing what they are doing for power and control and to destroy what we have so that they can have the kind of world they want. I don't think they really care about the poor and the masses and the minorities. I think they are basically using them to get what they want. That's what political correctness is all about. That's what the Frankfurt School started.

From what I have read, there are people making a conscious effort to create the kind of world our ancestors didn't want in America. They want the whole world run by an oligarchy of very wealthy, powerful people, and the rest of us will be slaves and serfs and peasants and peons. To do that, they have to destroy the white race and the middle class, and basically America and Europe. I think it's very conscious, and I don't think it has anything to do with helping anyone or wanting to right all of the wrongs of the past. It's very deliberate, and they're using a lot of good people who do want to right wrongs and correct things for their own purposes. I think that once they achieve what they want, a lot of people are going to be real surprised at what happens to them.

At the bookstore, I would pick up one book and that would lead to another. I read some things about the civil rights movement and I was so shocked. I couldn't believe some of the things that happened. It wasn't just a lot of wonderful people trying to solve terrible problems and injustices. When the civil rights marches were going on, I was a teenager and it all seemed so noble to me. And growing up in a very strong Christian household, it was "God loves us all equally"—which I still believe—but now as a mature woman, I'm starting to say, "Wait a minute, this was all a fraud!" I used to think that all the people who came rushing down from the North were wonderful Christian people or great Jewish liberals. That is what we were told by television and everything. But I have read that many of the people who went down there were paid to participate in this movement, and that many of them were disgusting people, foul-mouthed and totally immoral.

Even Martin Luther King, who was supposed to be the greatest saint that ever lived: what his life was really like and what he was really like and what the people around him were really like was disgusting. Some of the things I read were by black authors, so that made me feel like, well, at least it's not just some members of the Ku Klux Klan or something that are saying that. These are people who were actually part of his movement. I wondered why I had never heard about any of this before. It obviously was being kept from us deliberately.

I remember when I was young somebody saying Dr. King was a communist and everybody jumping all over him: "How could you say that, you awful person?" But then I read that John Kennedy called him to the White House and said, "You've got to get rid of your communist advisors," which King ignored. One of the books I read had a section by a black woman who saw what he was really like. Disgusting sexual practices, horrible! Not at all what you would expect from any Christian much less a minister. I think he may have started out as a sincere black Christian minister who really believed he could do some good, but he was used by people who realized what they could accomplish with him. From what I have read, a lot of it had to do with giving him all the women he wanted, particularly a lot of white women to go to bed with. The FBI file on Dr. King is being withheld from the public until the year 2028, I think it is. Why? What is in that file?

South Texas where I was living has many wonderful aspects to it. The cost of living is low and housing is reasonable, and while the summers are hot, the winters are mild, and there's no state income tax. But it got so I just didn't want to live there anymore. I wanted to go to New Hampshire or Montana or someplace, and that's why I ended up moving and taking a different job, because I wanted to get away to where people are more like me. This was about two years ago when I made my decision. I'm in Massachusetts now, in the central part of the state. But to my dismay, I'm finding that even up here, thousands of Hispanics are flooding in. I guess they came up, or are being brought up, to work in factories or something. I really don't know.

I love to travel. My goal is to see every state in the United States and to see every capital. I color them off on a map as I finish because I love America so much. Two years ago, I was going through Iowa. There was a big thing when I was there about how they are bringing in hordes of immigrants so that they can work in industries and agriculture. I went through the governor's mansion on a tour and I had a chance to meet the governor's wife. I said to her, "Thank you for taking me through your lovely home, and I appreciate the opportunity to meet you, and if I can say one thing to you it's for heaven's sake don't bring all these Hispanic people in. Everybody else is trying to get away from them. Why do you want to bring them in when you have a state that's ninety-eight percent white?" Her mouth dropped open and she stared at me and pushed me aside. I'm sure that she thought I had lost my mind. But I thought they had lost their minds to have a place where they didn't have any of them and then to bring them in on purpose.

I have two nephews. One is getting ready to go to college and the other one will be going to college in a couple of years. They are both bright, talented boys. But of course they're facing this "You can't get into our college because we have to have this number of blacks and this number of Hispanics and this number of whatever." There is a lot of discrimination against white people in favor of minorities at the present time, whether it is done formally or informally. I think that is bad, but I think also that much of what is being done is actually very cruel to minorities. If Jane Doe Minority or John Doe Minority could do well at a small teachers college and get a decent education and a good job, that's wonderful. But if you take that person and stick them at Harvard or Yale or Princeton or Stanford or Columbia and they can't do the work, it's cruel because they may well not be able to keep up and they will drop out. From what I understand, the minority dropout rate is huge in those kinds of places. These kids go to Harvard or Yale and they're built up like they're gods, and then a year or two later they come crawling home with their tails between their legs. They were set up for failure, and nobody doing this to them seems to care how humiliating and degrading it is to the minority children. And of course they couldn't care less about how unfair it is to deserving white children to be the victims of racial discrimination.

I had just had my fifty-third birthday. I've lived alone for years— my husband was killed in Vietnam. I've never been afraid of anything, but I've started to think, "What am I going to do when I am sixty and seventy and eighty and all by myself?" I don't want to live behind burglar bars and be afraid to go to the store for fear that some monster is going to beat me up and rape me and rob me. I am feeling my mortality, and a lot of that is tied into the fear of what is going on with other racial and ethnic groups and how that's changing our country and our communities. I've always felt safe because I was a nice person. If I met someone, I was always friendly with them. It didn't make any difference if it was a black janitor or a Hispanic bus driver or whatever, I was always very friendly and nice, and people always appreciated the fact that I treated them just like everybody else. But what's going on today, people don't care who you are or how nice you are or how unprejudiced you are. If you are in their sights and you're the wrong color, you're dead. And their turf is expanding rapidly. I keeping thinking, where can I go to be safe when I get older? I am thinking of moving to Maine. I think it is safe there still.

12   WHITE BOY

Glenn Douglas* is a college student from California.

I am twenty-one years old. I was born in Canada, in the province of Ontario. My father is a native-born Canadian. My grandfather emigrated from Scotland. My mother is Irish. She was born and raised in Ireland. My parents met while going to school in Canada. I have a sister three years younger than I am. My dad is a high school teacher. When I was five, we moved to California.

I was pretty religious growing up. I was an altar server in the Catholic Church for a few years, and I went to Catholic grade schools. I am glad I went to Catholic schools because they were really good. They emphasized reading and writing a lot and I was doing more advanced stuff in the fourth grade than I did in the public middle school and even in high school.

At the end of the third grade, my mother and my sister and I went to Ireland for the summer. We stayed with my grandparents, who have a beautiful house near the ocean. Ireland was like a fairy tale country—so different from what I had been used to in California. In California, my sister and I were never allowed to venture far from my parents' sight because they were worried about what might happen to us, but in Ireland the only thing my parents worried about was us being home on time to eat dinner.

My sister and I spent the whole summer roaming around the hills and the fields. We would be walking along the country road and cars would stop and people would start talking to us. They would know my mother. I thought it was really cool how close the community was there and how everybody knew each other and how everybody's family went back. Ireland was just a very close-knit, family-oriented place, and I really liked it a lot.

In hindsight, I think that summer was a very important time for me. It was really the start of my racial understanding. When I went back to California, I missed the farm animals, and I had to be careful again where I went. I was kind of changed because I had experienced a whole different side of the world that the kids I was going to school with had no idea existed. In California I didn't even know my next-door neighbors, where in Ireland I knew everybody. I just thought California was a dump compared to where I had been in the summer.

In Ireland where I was, it was all white. The closest thing to foreigners were people who were English or German. Over here in California, it is completely different. We have all different types of people. I very much preferred the environment where it was homogeneous—one race and one culture and a close-knit community. I am not saying that I immediately became what I would call a racialist or anything from that summer, but I do think that the Ireland trip sowed some seeds in my mind. I am really glad I went because it made me realize at a young age that America and California aren't the whole world, that there were very different places from what we have here. I went back to Ireland every summer for the next five years after that first visit. I always looked forward to the summer and enjoyed going back there.

I never really thought consciously in racial terms until I went to middle school where it was about sixty to sixty-five percent Mexican. There were also Filipinos and blacks in the school. I was made fun of and called "white boy" a lot. I was often beaten down by packs of Mexican or Filipino guys. I told teachers about it a few times, but they wouldn't do anything. They just kind of said, "OK, I'll talk to them," and nothing happened. I noticed everybody who was cool wore pants that were like five sizes too big and listened to rap. And there were a few girls I liked in the class, and they hung around with that type of people. My reaction to what I experienced was to kind of go along with the flow. I looked at my clothes and, you know, I was really uncool. I thought to myself, "Well, I've got to go shopping." My dad started saying, "Well, you want to be a Mexican now," but I wasn't really thinking in those terms. I just thought I was being fashionable.

For a while I guess you could say I turned into a wigger. [A wigger is a white person who dresses and takes of the manner of a black.] Most of my friends were Mexican. They taught me about "tagging," which is basically vandalizing, writing things everywhere.

I started buying markers and going to malls and tagging 'cause I thought that was what I was supposed to do. And I got into drugs. I was really going downhill. My parents were concerned, but they really didn't do anything.

After a while, I started to notice that the Mexicans hung together and had their thing, and the Filipinos and blacks hung together, and the whites, including me, were always trying to get into those groups. I started wondering, "Why aren't we doing our own thing?" So I gradually slipped away from the crowd I had been hanging with. In my school, there were really two main cultures, "rappers" and "rockers." About ninety percent of the kids were rappers. If you were white, that meant wearing baggy clothes and pretending to be Mexican or black. The rockers were kind of rebellious against that. They wore their hair long and listened to, like, Metallica and Guns N' Roses. I began to see a conflict where the rappers and rockers were struggling for power in the school. I kind of drifted into the rocker group. Even though we weren't using drugs all that much, we were called "stoners." Looking back on it, joining up with the rockers was the beginning of me trying to identify with my own kind.

I remember when the film *Braveheart* came out. I was really impressed with it and very inspired by it. I saw it with my father and he pointed out to me, "That's our ancestors up there on the screen." I started thinking, you know, Mexicans wear "brown pride" T-shirts to school and talk about who they are, and I am white and I've got a culture and a great history and I am proud of that. So I started to identify with white people a little bit more. It was fashionable to act ashamed of being white and I really couldn't relate to that anymore.

I started to notice huge double standards—how it is OK to be proud if you belong to any race but the white race. I noticed that I couldn't even talk about being white without being ridiculed, and it usually came from other whites, who said how wrong it was to have an affinity for your own kind. I spent all my time wishing I lived somewhere else but California, like Ireland or some place in Europe, where I imagined that they didn't have these kinds of problems, where you could just go to school and all you had to worry about was getting good grades.

When I was in high school, I grew my hair long and wore all black. I met another kid who became really my one and only friend during high school. He was heavily into death metal and black metal music. Him and I discovered Norwegian black metal and really got into that. That music really had a big influence on my behavior and way of looking at things. Black metal was obscure, little known music. At that time, you couldn't buy it in mainstream stores. The only way we got hold of CDs was through mail order. Me and my friend were the only ones who listened to it, so we felt kind of special, like it was our music, like it was made just for us. We spent our time together listening to black metal music in his house, or we'd go hiking somewhere, just wander off in the woods and just talk about whatever.

I'd describe black metal as very angry. It expresses disdain and disgust for modern society. Black metal bands use pagan imagery, European imaginary. Most of band members had long hair and they wore all black, or they might have some form of medieval armor and tall boots. They'd pose for pictures in forests with swords. All that appealed to us because, for one, it was sort of a white thing. What also made black meal so special to my friend and I was that the members of these bands seemed to be dead serious. In interviews, they would talk about overthrowing Christianity and returning to a Middle Ages-type European society. My friend and I spent time reading about pagan religion. I began to really have a hatred for Christianity because I thought, "Look what Christianity has done to us. It's disarmed our people and made us tolerate and embrace other races who bring us down." Being an alienated kid, black metal was just very appealing. If you have disdain for society and you don't feel like you belong, and you see somebody basically standing up for what you believe in, it just…I guess we were sort of reaching back into the past where life was better than the one we were living.

We listened a lot to a band called Burzum. It was a one-man band, really, a Norwegian guy named Varg Vikernes. He had a big impact on me. He would come out and say, "I do my own thing, and if anybody doesn't like it, I will kill them." As crazy as it might sound now, I really looked up to that. Vikernes referred to himself as a racialist pagan and a neo-Viking and he flirted with National

Socialist imagery. A lot of the black metal CDs had runes [ancient Germanic symbols] on them. Burzum and most of the other bands were from Norway. At the time, I didn't even know where Norway was in the world. I started reading about Norway and about European history, the Vikings in particular. It was my way of reaching toward my European roots—having some kind of identity.

During high school, I would seldom talk to anybody, and a lot of people seemed to kind of fear my friend and I because we were just considered so weird. That gave us a sense of identity. It made us stand out and feel kind of good. I continued to be picked on by Mexicans, but I started discovering ways of fighting back. On one occasion, a big Mexican walked by me and said, "Hey white boy." I simply turned around and said, "Hey spic." He went ultra dramatic: "What did you call me?" I just calmly told him that I had called him a spic. He looked me in the eye and I looked him right in the eye and did my best to give him the impression that I really didn't give a damn, and he backed off. I spent a lot of my time trying to learn how to intimidate people as best as I could because I felt that was the only way I could get by. I had nobody to back me up if I got in trouble.

In my classes in school, I noticed that the history of European people was always presented from a negative point of view. We always seemed to be talking about civil rights and the horrible things whites had done. When we were talking about WWII, all I learned was that the Germans were evil racists. The swastika was a Christian cross that had been twisted because Hitler worshipped the Devil. Literally, that's what I was taught in school. Even though I really didn't know anything about it, I had a hard time accepting that and I began to question it a little bit. I had a hard time believing that this evil empire was trying to take over the world. I also noticed how blacks were always referred to as African Americans, and there were Asian Americans. But we were always white with a small "w." And I thought, "Well, we came from Europe, so why aren't we referred to as European Americans?" I just kind of noticed that there was a double standard. I was never really upfront and challenged my teachers, though.

Teachers were always portraying a multicultural attitude as a virtue. But you have to remember that I had made trips to Ireland.

That was a very different environment and, to me, a much more preferable environment. I thought to myself, "Why do I like it so much in Ireland?" I decided that I wasn't alienated in Ireland because I was among my own kind. It was a white culture. It was a more family oriented culture, with roots, where people have a long and common history. It was also less built up. There weren't any big cities like where I was living. I began to think, "Well, imagine what the world would be like without having to mix with and tolerate other races." I imagined whites having our own living space.

I spent a lot of time reading on my own in high school. I would just pick books off library shelves. I think this was important for me. It taught me to be a questioner. It made me a little bit more intelligent, I like to think, than the average teenager who watches TV all day. My father bought me a H.P. Lovecraft [American fiction writer, 1890-1937] book for Christmas. I started reading him and thought he was a very interesting author. I learned that he wrote for a pulp magazine called *Weird Tales*, and I started reading other authors who wrote for that magazine. That's how I discovered Robert Howard, who is most well known for writing the Conan the Barbarian stories. The Conan stories had a big influence on me. Howard was certainly racial. He had strong Aryan characters. He described a brutal time where men had to fight to live, had to fight their way through the world. Killing people was not such a big deal. Almost every day was an adventure. The Conan stories went along with what I was listening to with black metal. All my heroes in the black metal scene talked about standing up for yourself, and I started to think, how can I stand up for myself and be more of a man? My friend and I started lifting weights.

I read the Lord of the Rings trilogy in about a month. I was really into Tolkien's world. In fact, I tried to convince myself that I was reading a history text and not an imaginary story. I looked back fondly to a European-type society where life was simpler. Not that I had a real understanding of it at the time, but I just thought the idea of living in a homogeneous environment where men were men and women were women and life was hard but closer to nature…well, it just seemed like a better way of living to me. I wished my life was more like that instead of being a kid stuck in multi-racial California where I couldn't feel free to be who I was and was alienated from everything.

During the last part of high school, I watched a movie called *Higher Learning* that featured a white kid who got taunted and beaten up and made fun of, and he got introduced to a couple of white power skinheads. That was really the first time I had heard about the whole white power movement, and that kind of intrigued me. I thought it would be great if I had some group that I could relate to; you know, that would stick up for me and be my extended family. I spent some time looking up these groups on the Internet, and I agreed with their racial policies. I discovered Tom Metzger and his group, WAR [White Aryan Resistance]. I started subscribing to the WAR newspaper—I was about seventeen then—and I started reading about the white power movement from their perspective, not from everybody else's. I came across a National Alliance sticker that someone had placed on the wall of a coffee shop. They sent me a book catalog and I began to read *The Turner Diaries* [by William Pierce] and books like this.

I began to have a distaste for the mass media. I'd go to a teen movie and always there would be blacks and whites together as friends. Actually, though, what really bothered me wasn't the racial mixing but just the fact that these movies put down white culture in every way you can think of. I was, like, "Wait a second. Who makes these movies and who decides who gets cast?" I heard that Jews owned the mass media, so I started thinking maybe they are responsible for these things I don't like. I had never thought much about Jews. I had been taught that they were always persecuted, but like every other kid I assumed that must be due to bigotry and people not being able to understand them. I thought, Jews are white people with just a different religion, so what's the big deal? But I gradually began looking into it and I realized that Christianity wasn't really the source of the degeneracy I was seeing around me. It was a part of it, but the main fact was that there was an alien race, the Jews, that was influencing us through the mass media. It was a gradual process, but I started to see how things fit together a little bit.

After high school, I went to a community college. To be honest with you, the first year I spent there I didn't take it more seriously than I did high school. I was basically getting C's. I saw that they had clubs for everybody but us. I thought, "Gosh, I better start a white club." They had a black student union and I wanted to do the same thing. I thought starting a white student club would be a great way to meet new people and add to our sense of community. So I talked to people on the board at school and read the constitution and found out how to do it. I outlined the club and everything, and put together a petition and got the required ten signatures.

Getting the petition signatures was very interesting. Some of the people I asked to sign were really excited, glad someone was thinking what they were thinking, and they said, "Oh yeah!" But some said, "You must be a racist." I said, "What do you mean?" They said, "Why would you want to start a white club?" I said, "Why would anyone want to start a black club?" Another student said calling it a white club is talking about skin color and that's wrong. These people had thoroughly taken in what they had been taught.

I got my signatures and the only thing left that I needed to do was get a faculty member to sponsor the club. But not one would do it. Every one of them I talked to tried to discourage me. They even lied to me. They were telling me, "Well, you can't do this," and I would pull out the rules and regulations and say, "It says right here any group can organize." They would say, "Well, this is really meant for minorities." I'd say, "It doesn't say it here, and anyway whites are a minority now in California."

It's almost like you go to college to get stupid. I took a sociology class where the professor was trying to tell me race was completely a socially constructed phenomenon. He said that there is just one human race and that we are all members of it. That's ludicrous. There are human races plural, just as there are different breeds of dogs. You can call them all dogs if you want to, but don't try to pretend a poodle is the same thing as a pit bull.

The way I see it, it is just natural for you to want to identify with your own race and socialize with your own race and reproduce your own race. You want to preserve your own race in the same way that someone wants to preserve the environment. But anybody who thinks as I do is called a racist, which, as it is defined today, means hating other races. But to me that isn't what a racist is. A racist is someone who acknowledges the obvious fact that there are significant differences between races that go beyond skin color. I'm talking about things like intelligence and tendencies toward certain ways of living.

A racist sees his or her race as an extended family. If you have a family of your own, you know that while you are friendly with your neighbors and you help them, when it comes down to it, your family comes first. You look out for your family and see that they are fed and clothed. You don't necessarily think your family is superior or better than all the other families around you in your neighborhood, and you don't deny your neighbors the right to exist, and you respect their space. But you do believe you have the right to your own house and your own property and to live your way. If your neighbor is always barging in and saying, "Hey, we are all one big family here," and saying that he really doesn't like you and is entitled to part of what you have and starts cluttering up your house and beating up your children, after a while you start to resent him. You want to reclaim your home, reclaim your life. I think, in a way, that is a good analogy to describe how what I would call true racists feel as members of the white race.

I have never had the chance to say this in any of my classes. As soon you raise your voice, they basically shut you up. I did write a paper criticizing multiculturalism and contradicting some of the things I was being taught, but I got a bad grade on it, not because I didn't do the research or back up my arguments or it was badly written. The professor simply didn't agree with me. I had the same thing happen on a paper I wrote criticizing feminism. I have learned to play the game a little bit better, however, and now I get pretty good grades. I don't have any problems in school now. I'm pretty much compromising myself to get my degree. I'm trying not to forget who I am and what I believe in, though.

After I graduate, I'd like to be a psychologist or psychiatrist, although I'm not really sure. I guess at the end of the day, first and foremost I am a white racialist. I feel obligated to help out my race in some way if I can. I just hope whites learn to organize and stand up for themselves, and I want to contribute to that. I love Ireland and I'd like to live there, and maybe someday I will. But in a way I don't like the thought of moving to Ireland because that seems like running away from the problems we face here. I have a girlfriend now and she's racially conscious. She wasn't when I first met her, so I guess I have influenced her in that regard. I'd like to have a family some day—you know, raise some kids. I don't want my children going through what I went through growing up, though. I'll do what I can to try to see that that doesn't happen.

13   NEWS WITHOUT JEWS

Alex Linder is thirty-five and has lived the past few years in Missouri after a decade in Washington, D.C. He operates an online white racialist news service called Vanguard News Network. His manner is energetic and direct.

I have a factual bias, you might say. I dislike anything or anybody that claims reality is one way when it's not. I don't like anything or anybody that gets between people and what is really going on. I consider myself a true conservative. True conservatism has to do with facts and limits. My mother's family are Christian Scientists and I was raised in that religion. Christian Science claims that disease is a product of bad thoughts. I don't believe that myself. I never did believe it. If you apply conservative principles, that's a ridiculous claim. Just like the idea that Jesus walked on water. I am a white racist because racism is simply factual reality. And by the way, "racist' and "racialist" are interchangeable terms to me. Really, I don't label myself—"I'm a white nationalist," "I'm a pan-Aryan," whatever. Labeling is for the other guy. I don't worry about labeling. I just call myself white and know that I want to live in a white neighborhood, that's it.

I was born in Madison, Wisconsin and lived there until the fourth grade. I then lived in California, Illinois, and finally Utah, where I graduated from high school in 1984. My father is of German background and my mother's side of the family is English and Swiss. We weren't rich, but thanks to my parents' hard work I enjoyed a comfortable, stable, middle-class childhood. My parents' stability and love for each other and me and my siblings showed me how a solid white family and society can work.

I didn't really grow up around blacks much at all. I went to suburban schools and was taught the same b.s. that everybody else is about race not existing and the rest of it. I basically swallowed the individualist bias they were pumping at me that we had to be color-blind. I do recall one incident that suggested to me that blacks are not like whites. I was about eight or nine. My family went to Magic Mountain down in L.A. It's an amusement park with big roller coaster rides. We were in line waiting to go on a gondola that went back and forth and two black teenage couples cut in front of us. My father isn't a shrinking violent and so when we got up to the front of the line, he said to the guy running the gondola, "These people cut in line. We were here before they were."

At that point, those fucking little niggers starting cursing and bitching and complaining. I remember one of the black girls saying, "I hope you fall off halfway across!" I was totally taken aback. I remember thinking, "These people are not like us. There is a fundamental difference." It is like the scene in [the novel] *The Turner Diaries* where the niggers are pissing in the river. Jefferson said that the two races equally free can't live together under the same government and he was right. We are just different breeds of animals.

Growing up, I read a bunch of Mencken [iconoclastic journalist prominent in the 1920s, '30s, and '40s, H.L. Mencken], and his stuff seemed perfectly attuned to the way I think and what I find amusing and worthwhile. I decided that I wanted to spend my life creating the kind of joy you get when you read good Mencken or O'Rourke [contemporary political and cultural satirist, P.J. O'Rourke] or [Mark] Twain.

I went to Pomona [College], which is pretty good liberal arts school in Claremont, California. Generally, fairly well off liberal people go there. Since I had decided I was going to become a writer, I wrote for the school paper. I was co-opinions editor. I wrote some editorials and they started getting pissed at me. One was about AIDS. There had been a *Newsweek* cover with snapshots of about a hundred people who died of AIDS on it. Of course, it was "Semitically correct." Note that I used [syndicated columnist Joseph] Sobran's term, Semitically correct, not politically correct, so the accent is on the Jews, who have set up the terms of the system.

Anyway, I pointed out in my AIDS article that these *Newsweek* guys were totally misrepresenting reality. They showed six-year-old kids and ninety-five-year-old grandmothers instead of a bunch of loose-assed, disgusting fags who slept with thousands of people

apiece and already had forty or fifty venereal diseases before they got
AIDS. *Newsweek* was just Jews lying about reality and I hate people
who lie about reality. The difference between me and other
conservatives, though, is that it wasn't enough for me to point out
what they were doing in a boring footnote style, what I call
remonstrating. I made it kind of funny and pointed and barbed. I also
wrote a column called "Of (f) Color," just making fun of the term "of
color." They used to be colored, then they were Negroes, then they
were blacks, then African Americans, and now they are people *of*
color. I mean, "ain't social change grand." Another article I wrote
was after a speech on campus by [Holocaust survivor] Elie Wiesel. I
said that the best way to "never again" was for Jews to stop whining
all the time.

Well, they got all mad. The college administrators denounced me
and all the deans and everybody. They all signed a statement saying,
"Mr. Linder is an example of how far we have to go." Then they
started fighting among themselves. The faggots starting writing in,
"The administration didn't say a thing when Mr. Linder was
criticizing the homosexual community, but the minute he touches
blacks, they just go nuts!" They held a couple of college senate
meetings to decide whether to kick me out of school, although that
finally died down.

My editor was a Jewish feminist and my co-opinions editor was a
Kennedy-esque liberal. They did a number of intrigues behind my
back and sprung stuff on me. The co-opinions editor was promoted to
senior co-opinions editor over me and got to make all the decisions.
They let a mulatto friend of a girl I knew write in my space. I was
pretty much shut out of writing for the college paper even though my
articles had drawn more student response than anything in its history.

I just shook my head and laughed at how intolerant and really
hateful and vicious all these people were. When I was co-opinions
editor, I had never in any way tried to suppress anyone who wrote for
me. In fact, I had more liberals than conservatives writing for me.
My attitude was, let everyone speak and let the reader sort out what's
best. I came to see the left as completely anti-democratic. They
absolutely hate freedom of speech. They want to win and they don't
care by what means they win. They will do *anything* to you. If you

aren't prepared to fight on those terms, you might as well give it up. One thing that stayed with me was how when all this hubbub was going on, a lot of people came up to me on the side and said, "Thanks, man, for saying what you did and standing up." I realized if you display a fighting spirit or courage, people will come to you.

What really struck me in college is that there is no institutional support at all for anybody who is white, traditional, and conservative. It is rigged to help anybody who is liberal or a minority, and particularly anyone who is Jewish. There is resistance to anyone who is on the right. The place is completely geared to furthering what is basically the Jewish agenda, which is ninety percent of liberalism. Everything is geared in that direction—the courses, the books used in the courses, the faculty picked to teach, all of it. The Jews have [the campus organization] Hillel, and they get funding to put out their little newsletters. For the right, there is nothing. I have unlimited contempt for the people who administer colleges. They are very weak and unprincipled people. I consider them worse than Mexicans, the absolute lowest. I despise Mexicans. They are an off-brand people.

Stupid conservative parents send their kids to these schools. All they see is Stanford or whatever, and that is what they buy. They don't look at what kind of books the students actually read there and what is actually taught. These parents pay these people $20,000 or $30,000 a year to indoctrinate their children. They just trust, and they put their faith in the wrong thing. I majored in international relations. Basically, I read a bunch of Institute for Policy Studies stuff from the communist [Richard] Barnett. I've probably read every book he has ever written. I heard crap about Vietnam I didn't believe.

I was ready to drop out when I was a sophomore. I figured I would never spend my own money on this, so why was I wasting my parents' money? But I was playing on the baseball team and got into writing for the paper and I enjoyed that, and I had a lot of friends there, so I stayed. Conservative parents are just propping up a system that has disdain for them. They figure I'm getting my son a degree from wherever. They think they are buying a name, but in most cases they aren't. Unless it's Harvard or Yale, I don't think that the name is worth much. Being a Pomona graduate hasn't gotten me shit.

College was fun, but if I had children I would never spend that kind of money on it. It's just not worth it. It's four years of your life at a time when you are at your strongest physically. Is that really what you want to buy with all that money? There might be a case for it if you are in the hard sciences, which are harder to corrupt, but for anything in the liberal arts, I think there are better alternatives. You could find someone who is the best at what you want to do and copy off them, or go directly to them and try to get them to teach you. And now with the Internet, you can figure out what is going on and teach yourself. That's what I would say at thirty-five.

Just before I graduated from Pomona, perusing the stacks at the library I discovered the *American Spectator* magazine and loved it. I thought, "This is *funny*, like Mencken's stuff was!" In one of the issues, there was an ad for an intern, so I applied, and they actually gave me the position. I was absolutely thrilled. "Boy, it is going to be fantastic to work for the *Spectator*," I thought to myself. "It is somewhat satirical, more than the *National Review* is, and it's got great writers. Whatever I wanted to do in college, mocking and all that, I am going to be able to do at the *Spectator*. I am going to carry on the Mencken tradition. I'm going to criticize everybody, take on the world. I'm going to be free!"

So I worked at the *Spectator* and I did enjoy it. It was mutually good for me and for them. They said I did a great job. But after the internship ran out, there was only one editorial position open and they gave it to someone else. The guy they gave it to was very qualified, though.

The founder and editor-in-chief of the *Spectator* is R. Emmett Tyrrell. I literally trembled when he walked in the room because I had so much respect for him. One day, I showed him my "Of (f) Color" article. I'll never forget this because it was a turning point in my life. He read it over and got a long face and said, "Well, we are very careful about this sort of thing." Now, I make a distinction between people being little and being big. Mencken, with his accomplishments, deserves the title of big. Tyrrell pulled up short where Mencken would *never* have pulled up short. I thought to myself, "He's little, and I'm going to do whatever I can to be big, because I'm not afraid of whatever he's afraid of." Tyrrell is a really good guy, but that is the judgment I made about him when I was twenty-two years old.

After leaving the *Spectator*, I went on to the National Journalism Center, a journalist training school in D.C. After that, I worked for [conservative syndicated columnists] Evans and Novak doing research for them. I saw that there was no way I was going to be able to get paid to write anything approaching the truth about Jews or coloreds in the professional conservative industry. So I went to work at Phillips Publishing. They do newsletters for companies, that sort of thing, desktop publishing. I saw it as uninspiring but honorable work.

After three years with Phillips, I started my own company doing the same thing. I was successful and it was profitable financially, but I was bored as hell writing about computers and health care. I just had to do it my own way and see what happens. So I quit what I was doing, broke up with my girlfriend, and, after a decade in the D.C. area, went back to the Midwest. In 2000, a partner and I started Vanguard News Network, and that's what I am doing now, and it's been great.

I became fully racist by living in D.C., which is, except for maybe Detroit, *the* blackest city in America. I saw that if you are going to embrace color-blind individualism the way the Jews that control both the liberals and the conservatives say you should, it is white genocide. Whites cannot live around people like this, period. What you'll eventually get is South Africa or Zimbabwe, where whites are completely destroyed as a race. Marion Berry, the mayor of Washington when I was there, was busted for crack, and he is the kind of person blacks elect over and over when they are left alone to vote. There is something general going on with these people. It's not individual at all. I came to realize that if you stick to individualism and you refuse to generalize, it's going to kill your race.

During this time, I read a book by John Murray Cuddihy called *The Ordeal of Civility*, and it blew my mind probably more than anything I'd read in my whole life. It's very hard to find that book now because the Jews have suppressed it. The Cuddihy book tracks the hostility of the Jewish intellectual giants, Freud, Marx, and Levi Strauss. It shows the hate for the white race that underlies their supposedly objective theories. Marx, for example, says, well, yes, the

Jew may look like a scheming, dirty, nasty little creature, but that is just a class thing. Once we go through these revolutions all that will disappear. And Freud says that if a white person is reserved, dignified, private, and classy, he's repressed. *You're* the sick ones, not us. And so on. These theories are aimed at destroying us. The Cuddihy book tied together a thousand little things I had noticed about Jews and set them into a pattern.

Kevin MacDonald's books are good, too. I especially recommend his book, *The Culture of Critique*. There is not a better book to read if you want to understand how America got to be the way it is and, closer to home, why your son is a wigger and your daughter is a lesbian and your neighbors are Mexicans and Filipinos. The neoconservatives will criticize the Frankfurt school, but they will always refer to them as German or European, never as Jews. The Cuddihy and MacDonald books are the kind of stuff you should be taught in college, but you never are because you are paying money to exactly the same people who are promoting these race-killing theories.

I knew coming out of college that the left lies about everything. Everything they say is factually untrue. Equality of racial intelligence, whatever it is, they are lying about it. My problem was I made the illogical leap to conclude that if the left is lying about everything, the right must be telling the truth. And a lot of what the right says is the truth, but not everything, that's the big point. Conservatives don't tell the truth if it conflicts with the Jewish agenda, simple as that. "Race doesn't exist" and extreme egalitarianism—the Jews have been pushing that dogma for a hundred years and will cut anybody out of the loop who disagrees with it. The Jews are big liars, and one of their biggest lies is about what America was founded to be. They put out there that the United States was founded as a place that is purely about some ideas, democracy and equality, and where race and history and the background of people don't matter. That's just garbage, the big lie. It is not good for Jews that whites know their roots and their own true history. It's good for Jews if whites think, "Oh, anybody can become an American and we ought to have open borders."

You may think, "But [black intellectual] Thomas Sowell never did anything wrong. He's screwed if you adopt racism." And that is true. But unlike the conservatives, I admit the cost of my position—it screws some blacks. But the conservatives never admit the *huge* cost of their position. Whole countries get screwed. Like, to name three, Zimbabwe, South Africa, and, in another fifty years, the United States. Conservatives never admit that failing to treat blacks as a general group is the way to the cultural and racial death of white people. Conservatives won't tell you that because they make too much money off of what they are telling you. Or they're like [pro football player and Vice Presidential candidate] Jack Kemp. America has to die because Jack Kemp showered with some black men. Some black guy soaped Jack's back and I'm supposed to ignore a million black-on-white crimes every year. Sure, I'll do that, Jack, just for you.

What I came to see, and this is the big story here, is that conservatives are a fake opposition. They are fake in the sense that they won't take on the most vital questions confronting us: race and Jews. That's the fault line right there and they won't cross it. If something touches on the truth about race or is critical of Jews, they won't go near it. I guess I was naïve, but I figured that something that is obviously true would make people on the right stand up for it. Well, it's not like that. As Sobran pointed out in his pamphlet *How I Was Fired by Bill Buckley*, it is all just a game to conservatives, just a way to make a living. But it's not like that to me. It's blood, complete blood. If you're a writer and you're pulling your punches, if you are writing things you know aren't true, if you're withholding the truth, what are you? How can you have any self-respect at all? I got into writing to be Mencken. You've got the *American Spectator* that is supposed to be the heir of Mencken—they have a dummy of Mencken sitting there in their office, for Christ's sake!—and you're afraid??

I had learned what liberalism is by living through my editor and co-opinions editor in college conspiring behind my back and totally shitting me over. Then I learned what conservatism is by working at the *American Spectator* and seeing that they were just as scared as the weakling liberal college administrators were about anything that touched on race. I mean, what needs mocking more in our society than niggers? It's fucking ridiculous. You can't read word one about them that is disrespectful. Just today, I was online reading some black guy writing an opinion column about an Oliphant cartoon [political cartoonist, Pat Oliphant]—"Oh, that is racism!" Racism is anything or anybody opposed to the black agenda. Blacks take that directly from the Jews. An anti-Semite is simply somebody who is opposed to any item on the Jewish agenda. You oppose a Jew and you are an anti-Semite, it doesn't matter what it is about.

Blacks and the Jews have these terms they stick on anybody that doesn't go along with them and the right just plays along. I'm not doing that. I'm the true heir to Mencken. I'm not pulling punches. The conservatives pull their punches. They won't criticize blacks. Now, what could be more ludicrous than Al Sharpton and Jesse Jackson? Jesse Jackson is a nigger extortionist. Everybody in America knows that. You're supposed to be a conservative journalist following the line of Mencken and you don't say that in a crude, crass, nasty, and direct way? If you don't say it like that, then what are you?

Plus it takes the joy out of it to write cautious, coded, weak little trivial things. People don't want that. They want what we're doing at VNN, which is full of joy and slurs and truth. Slurs and the truth go together. To call someone an African American when he's a nigger? I refrain from calling Thomas Sowell a nigger, but I don't refrain from calling niggers niggers. [Conservative columnist] George Will wrote a column the other day about yet another great black guy who pulled himself up by his bootstraps. It's just stupid. I spit on them all. People are responding to what we're doing at VNN because it's clear that we are free. Something that is free has a distinct aroma and the conservatives don't have it.

The basic idea of Vanguard News Network is that it is news without Jews. It is an online newspaper. Its purpose is to do something daily that's carefully edited, reliable, pro-white, and anti-Jewish, with absolutely no Jewish participation at any point in the process. The American public understands there is something wrong with the media, that it is very biased, but they don't understand exactly what it is that is wrong. The conservatives who pretend to tell them, gutless clowns like Brent Bozell and Reed Irvine, will only go so far as to say the media is biased, which a child of three can see after watching Dan Rather for five minutes. What these people won't tell you is *why* the media is biased and *in whose interest* it's biased. It's biased because it is owned and controlled by Jews and serves their racial interests. VNN says that openly, forthrightly, and explicitly daily. Whatever attractiveness we have is attributable to that. We don't have as many readers as some of the big-name conservative sites, but we are going in the right direction and we are going to pass them eventually.

We have people who contribute original articles, opinion pieces, book reviews, cartoons, whatever, and we post those. I edit the things people submit. People also feed me links to news articles they think I might be able to use. We do a kind of *ju jitsu* on the Jewish media: their reporters write articles for the various newspapers and wire services, and then we pull the articles we want and link them but with our own spin. We call our introductions "spintros." An example of what we might do, a guy on our side might write up an article on a National Alliance demonstration and at the same time we'll link to the *Washington Post* description of the same thing. The idea is to create an alternative medium that is free of Semitic bias. It mostly comes down to selecting the right articles and presenting them in the right way. There are people working with me, but it is all done over the Internet. People from all over the country chip in writings and suggest articles to spin. We can't afford to pay anybody. Basically, VNN takes one monomaniac with a computer to do it, and that's me.

We are saying stuff on VNN you can't really find anywhere else. And it's not just that we are racists and reliable that attracts people. We're aggressive and people hunger for that, they love that. People sense that we really believe what we say, and they don't sense that when they read libertarians and conservatives. People see their stuff is just hackwork. There's a spiritual difference between us and the others. And we're funny. You can't get genuine humor any more because it is censored. It's dangerous. You can't make fun of Jews and "Mexcrement," but we do it all the time. We subject them to ridicule. We don't remonstrate, we ridicule. Anything can be destroyed by ridicule.

We aim to destroy Jewish control of the United States. And we are going to reveal and destroy the fake opposition in the form of conservatives and libertarians. True conservatism is racist. The people who are presented to us today as conservatives are not truly conservative. Every day since we started, we have been saying what they won't say. We point out their financial interest in keeping the truth from people. And we are doing the same thing to libertarians. We are going to make it clear that white nationalism is the only real opposition to the Jewish tyranny. The rest of what is going on is just a game. The two major political parties are both racial egalitarians selling the idea that race doesn't matter. Of course it matters.

We aren't considered respectable because respectability is defined by the Jews who control things as not mentioning Jewish power and not criticizing Jews as Jews. Conservatives will criticize the left or liberals or atheists or secular humanists, but never, never, NEVER will they point out the Jewish roots of these things. We point that out every single time. That is the fundamental difference between us and the rest of them. That is the market niche my partner and I saw. The only thing limiting us is distribution. If we could get our stuff on newsstands, people would buy it right up. But the Jews control news dissemination everywhere but on the Internet, and they are trying to get control of that. Except on the Internet, Jews control which writers and artists have access to the public.

If you are going to take on the Jews, you can't do just what you do and leave it at that. You have to do every other thing, too. You have to do printing and promotion and distribution. I come from trade publishing and I know how hard it is to get a couple thousand of something out. It takes a lot of money and a lot of time. But on the Internet, I just put it out there and anybody can read it. So the Internet has been a real godsend.

We take donations at VNN, but you wouldn't do this for the money. I had to do it for my soul. I know that sounds ridiculous, but that's the truth of it. I wasn't going to fucking die without taking my shot at it. VNN has allowed me to do something that's fulfilling and it proves that people want to read what I write. Now it is purely a question of whether the Jews can shut us down. What we do would be illegal in Europe. They'd bust in here and crack my head and take the computer. Jews believe Jews should be legally beyond criticism. That's a fact. They withhold from the American public that people in Europe are being arrested for writing books with views of history that the Jews won't tolerate or putting something critical of Jews on the Internet. Do you ever see the *New York Times* write about that?

What the Jews are trying to do right now is insert the concept of hate speech into the public mind. They get hate speech opposed to free speech and get the public asking, "Is this hate speech or is this free speech?" When the Jews get that way of looking at it in place, then they can silence the speech they don't like by calling it hate speech. Jews are very clever, you have to give them that. Their terms preclude any debate. You can't oppose any item on the Jewish agenda without being medically or morally ill. If you oppose their position on race, you're a racist; fags, you're a homophobe; women, you're a misogynist. If you are an environmentalist and want to stop immigration, it's "the greening of hate." I think one of their greatest crimes is what they've done to women through feminism. Most college-educated women think in feminist terms without realizing it. It's sad.

Jews want to win. They don't necessarily want blood to flow, but they will go to that if necessary. They are fighting us as a race and most people aren't conscious of that. At VNN, we're making them conscious of it.

Marxists like [Johns Hopkins University professor] Mark Crispin Miller say the media are all owned by corporations, that that's the way to understand the media. Newspapers all over the country have declining circulations. So how come these big corporations don't hire people who could build revenue? I could do it a lot better than the people who are running these big city papers. I know what people actually want to read. But they wouldn't publish it for the same reason they produce agit-prop movies—to brainwash white people. If we had a few million dollars we could do everything [media conglomerate] Viacom does except it would be non-niggerish. We'd produce white novels, white films, even white clothes.

The other races are encouraged to identify with their own people and to promote their racial interests, whereas we are called haters if we do it. Conservatives might point that out, but they'd be very careful and cautious about it. We do it straight out and we laugh when we do it. That indicates that we are free. People get that. That spirit comes across. People think, "These guys aren't scared of the Jews. They're not worried about them. They don't measure what they say against some kike's reception of it." When people see us being free, they start to feel freer themselves. That's why I want my name on this. I want my name used because openly speaking it is part of the whole deal, not only for me but for everybody. This "I'm Otto 94" doesn't make it. We need to move forward to a brighter future, and you don't do that with a bunch of anonymous people. They can say whatever they want to say about me. I don't care. They are going to have to put a bullet in my chest if they intend to stop me. I'm not fucking stopping. I don't have any money. I guess I have a lot of reasons to be unhappy. But I can honestly say I am completely happy and completely fulfilled. This is exactly what I am able to do and was meant to do and was trained to do. I should be doing it for some major media outlet, but the situation is such that I can't really do that. So I have to make my own way.

14   ANGRY WHITE WOMAN

Mary Rowland is thirty-three and single and lives in the foothills of the Sierra Nevada mountains in northern California. She is self-employed, operating a business out of her home.

Until a couple of years ago, I lived in southern California, so my socialization was all in that area of the country. I was raised a liberal and was a liberal activist in my twenties. I was primarily involved with conservation issues, but sometimes that would prod me into getting involved with other causes, like Indian rights. If they had a dump a mile from an Indian reservation, I might write a letter to the editor or something pointing out that this was environmental racism.

My first movement out of a strictly liberal position was around the issue of overcrowding. We have had so much population growth that the quality of the environment has declined. It became clear to me where the overcrowding problem was coming from, and that was Hispanic immigration from Mexico. There's hardly any European immigration now, so that isn't really an issue. But I decided it wasn't possible to say, "OK, let's stop immigration from non-white countries and keep immigration from Europe." So I started speaking out and writing about stopping all immigration, and again, it was from a conservation angle.

It wasn't long and my fellow conservation activists started pushing me away and whispering "racist." They'd say things like, "Isn't your position the same as [former Ku Klux Klan member and alleged racist] David Duke's?" I knew virtually nothing about David Duke at that time, but I got the basic idea. People started shunning me, and I got to be pretty much on their hit list. I realized from that experience that for the liberal crowd multiculturalism takes precedence over everything else, including the quality of the environment. Things finally got so uncomfortable for me that I resigned from my position on the board of the conservation organization I was in.

The immigration issue is what got me looking more at cultural and racial matters, and that led to the development of my own racial consciousness and racialism. For one thing, I noticed that when you look at the people who promote conservation in this country, they are predominately European Americans. I also started noticing things like in San Jose they replaced the Liberty Bell with a statue of Montezuma, the Aztec emperor. I thought about how in wars the conquerors start changing the street names and tearing down the reputation of the conquered people's founders. I realized that I was seeing that happen in my own country. So I started being concerned about the bigger picture. My kids, if I ever have them, are they going to be welcome in this country? Their forefathers died to secure this country for them. Are they going to walk around like they are strangers, like they are aliens here? I started asking questions like that.

I also saw what was happening in my own neighborhood. In a period of about five years, whites went from like eighty percent to about thirty percent. It had been a lower-middle income community with a lot of older people, but as soon as Mexicans started moving in, things started really breaking down. Young minority families moved in, and as soon as their kids hit their teen years, they began robbing people's houses and mugging old people, and so all those who could afford to move did.

I had to deal with racial harassment against me. I was a young woman with blond hair and blue eyes. I'd be walking down the street in my own neighborhood and a group of Mexicans would make sexual and racial comments to me. Or I'd be walking down the street and there would be black guys loitering on the side of the street, and one of them would say, "Hey baby, once you go black you'll never go back." There were other incidents where they wouldn't make a racial comment, but they would follow me and try to intimidate me, or they would be walking on the street and I would be walking the other way and they would spread out so I couldn't get by. I would have to walk way around them. It got to the point where I felt unsafe.

One of the defining moments for me in deciding that I was going to move away was what happened to this young sixteen-year-old white boy. He was about six feet tall with blond hair and blue eyes.

He was kind of a wigger, though. The first day he and his mom moved into the community, he was chased down by five Mexicans. They cornered him and said, "We don't like white boys around here." He talked his way out of it, but it was a frightening experience. What was happening in the neighborhood was a kind of ethnic cleansing of whites. They start ethnically cleansing you when they become maybe thirty percent of the population. They start harassing your kids. I started getting really agitated all the time and I knew I had to leave. I would come home and see in the pool of the complex I was in thirty Mexican kids and one little white girl. I just wanted to get out of there.

What really gets to me is how they say people are racists because they have never experienced diversity. The vast majority of racialists I know have experienced diversity first hand and that is it why they became racialists. I don't dislike people as individuals. It is the collective effect that their group has on my people and my culture that concerns me. If we are replaced by Mexicans, it's going to look like Mexico here and be like Mexico. I believe that the Mexican people and everyone else have a right to exist. But I also believe I should have a place where my kids can grow and prosper and not be forced to listen to "booga-booga" music and have black boys crammed down their throats. You can't even turn on the television and watch a commercial without hearing the sound of a black male singing or doing a voice-over. Our kids are being turned into wiggers. That is what they are being taught in place of the culture that made whites the most civilized and prosperous people on earth.

I remember one thing I did before I left southern California and moved up here that marked a turning point for me. I never had the nerve to do anything like it before because I was raised to be a nice, cooperative community member and somebody who doesn't make waves. I used to go to a Barnes & Noble bookstore and look at their bargain shelf. One time, I saw a book titled *101 Redneck Jokes*. I walked up the manager and I said, "Sir, do you have any nigger joke books?" He looked at me shocked. "No!" And then I handed him the joke book and said, "Well, then you shouldn't have this one."

How do you transmit your way of life and good values to your children? You promote good healthy cultural activities. You teach your children their ethnic heritage, their music. I was never taught the history of my people, the Celts. I've come to understand that a lot of who and what I am has to do with who they were a thousand years ago. The educational establishment makes it sound as if average Europeans who migrated here were the elite. The elite, much of the time, were not kind. They weren't even kind to their own people. But Europeans who came here weren't all elite. Many of my people—Scots and Irish—came here literally in chains or as indentured servants. They had done something considered criminal or got into debt and they were sent here to work off their debt to society. But they got through it, and they and their descendents went on to do great things.

Everybody who is white is pegged as being responsible for black slavery. For one thing, a very small percentage of the Southern landowners were slave owners. And besides that, the Moors, who were part black, enslaved my people, and the Mongols attacked Europe and enslaved my people when they had the opportunity. When they talk about the Indians, I'll talk about the Mongols. I'm not going to feel guilt for anything, not any more.

Today, our kids are learning about African history, and when they teach about European history they teach about slavery and other negative things designed to harm the self-esteem of white children. Whatever is on television or in the paper or anywhere else that's mainstream, and especially what is taught to our kids in schools, is presented in a negative context. For example, there's our war with the Indians. What they don't point out is that basically it was a military war with the Indians. The people I identify with aren't the soldiers. I identify with the pioneers, the people who were trying to live in peace. Maybe their wagon trains or their homes were attacked and the wife had her throat slit and their baby was stolen. They don't stress that the Europeans were industrious and inventive people, or that they developed great technology or created this or that vaccine. No, they must tell people that evil "Whitey" spread disease on purpose to kill Indians. They try to make it sound like white people, the most tolerant people on earth, are inherently evil and inherently anti-conservation and so on. I used to passively accept this kind of stuff. After a while, though, I started becoming really fed up. They pushed me the other direction. I realized that this culture promoted racism against whites, not vice versa.

There's good and bad with my people, so am I supposed to only identify with them when it comes to negative things? I am going to identify with positive things and I am going to stand up for my people, white people. When I was at my friend's house yesterday, I came across an article about a group called the European American Issues Forum. A reporter from a San Francisco newspaper wrote in the first sentence, "Oh, here's a group of people who say that they, as white people, are discriminated against." And then right after that sentence, she wrote, "Yes, the people who came here and exterminated the Indians." That's what she put in the article! I thought to myself when I read that, "When you talk about blacks, are you going to say these are the people whose ancestors were cannibals?"

We *do* live in a racist society. It's just that we're the only acceptable victims of it. I feel like a war of extermination is being conducted against us, I really do. They want to kill us kindly. They want you to marry an Asian and have a half Asian baby. They want me to marry a black and have mulatto babies. If I have kids, they are going to be white and they are going to be raised in a white community. They are not going to be raised in a multicultural community. I don't want anybody telling my kids at a young age that they are bad people and that their ancestors were dishonorable.

I'm thinking now that white people need a separate area where we can reproduce and live amongst our own and practice our traditional cultures. I'm not talking about a situation where it is like, "We claim this area for Aryans and anyone who tries to come in we're going to shoot you." It's more like people all moving to the same area. I'm planning to leave California next year. It's nice now where I am, but I want to leave while I am still young instead of when I am old and it's unbearable, when, to be blunt, the Mexicans move up here. We are already getting graffiti. There are a lot of beautiful natural places here and some lovely little towns, but they are coming up here and spraying their scrawl on everything in sight and vandalizing our schools. It's terrible.

Robert S. Griffin

This morning, it was reported in the paper that "hate flyers" were found in—I don't remember which state it was. I think the flyers were the ones the National Alliance distributes that say, "White people are an endangered species." Somebody does something as innocuous as that somewhere and I find out in California the next day. But most people didn't find out about what happened in Cincinnati, where about three hundred blacks blocked off a street and started pulling white people out of their cars and beating them up. The media always tries to cover up things like that. The people who control what we read and see on television in this country don't want white people to wake up. Hate knows no color—hate's not just a white thing. All racially aware white people aren't haters. What I am about isn't hate. I'm about love for my people and the heritage they have passed down to me to preserve and enhance.

I am a white separatist, not supremacist. I prefer to be around my own folk and practice my own folkways. That does not mean I am a bad person. In fact, I am basically a warm-hearted and generous person. I simply direct my love toward my own people in the same way other races do toward their own people. I will no longer be made to feel guilty for that. That doesn't mean I won't have a working relationship with someone outside my race, but that is all it will be. When you are a racialist, you can't have interracial friendships or love relationships and still be consistent. At least I can't.

I would like to have a family and children, but it is tough to find an appropriate man given my racialist perspective. There just aren't many men who see things as I do. And even if I found one of them, or at least someone who could accept me for who I am, there are all the other qualifications they must meet. I have very high standards around the way men think about women and the way they treat them and whether they are goal-oriented or not. A man I would marry would have to be hardworking and not an alcoholic or take drugs. I used to smoke but I quit, and I now I won't even accept smokers. So it's tough. And needless to say, the man I have children with will have to be white. I never bought the idea of interracial relationships that Hollywood is selling so hard to young people. Even before I was racially conscious, I never considered an interracial relationship. I simply wasn't attracted to non-whites, and on some level I knew it

134

was wrong despite having been raised to seek out and befriend minorities. Continuing the white race is a non-negotiable for me. I feel a strong moral obligation to have white children and make up for the feminist who has none.

Sometimes I wonder if what I have been through around race has taken my humanity away from me some and made me tougher to be around, which could be getting in the way of meeting a good man. Maybe if there weren't such immigration and multicultural overkill I would be the compassionate, generous person that I want to be toward everyone. All this has made me rougher around the edges. I mean, now I'll see a story about Jose Fuertes and his thirteen kids no longer having anywhere to live because there was a fire and they were burned out of their two bedroom apartment and I don't go, "Oh, how sad" like most people. I go, "My God, thirteen people?! Deport them all!!" Had Jose only had one child and his entire country wasn't moving in on us, I would feel compassion for his and his peoples' plight.

When I was in Frisco last week, I was looking at the architecture and I thought, "This a beautiful place." But look who is going to inherit it. My people built this country, and now these people have come in and my people are expected to put out the welcome mat and teach them how to take the reins of this society. They don't want to have anything to do with our culture, but they want to benefit from the society and infrastructure we created, all the while calling us names and accusing us of racism. Well, yeah, now I am a racist, Jose! If they say we were here first, this is Aztlan [the name Mexicans give to the Southeast United States], my attitude is, if you want it back I'm going to scorch the entire state and you can have it back the way it was when you were here—dirt, clay, and leaf huts. I know that maybe sounds harsh, but that is how I've become.

I can't say that I'm completely happy right now, but I'm not totally unhappy either, because I'm out in the country and not in the midst of the multicult cesspool as I was before. I was very unhappy in the city. But I know they will soon be "coming up the hill" toward me. I'm going to leave the state. Hopefully, my moving to a snowy, economically depressed area will keep them at bay.

I just want to live a normal life, preferably with a family, but if I can't have that, a life with good friends in a community where I feel safe and I'm free to walk down the street without looking over my shoulder. I just want to be able to express pride in my people and admiration for our white ancestors and to continue their traditions without minority harassment and interference. When I am really old, I want to live in peace instead of like those old people in the neighborhood where I used to live who are eighty-ninety years old without the energy or the money to escape.

15   RAISING HONORABLE WHITE CHILDREN

Ken and Elizabeth Gordon* live in New Hampshire and have four children, two boys and two girls, ranging in age from seven to fifteen. The family lives on three acres of land, where the children tend to the many chickens and goats. Both Ken and Elizabeth are university educated, Ken graduating from an Ivy League school and Elizabeth getting her degree from a public university on the West Coast. Ken works as an actuary. Elizabeth was in investments before leaving that career to be a full-time homemaker and focus her energies on homeschooling the children. "There is nothing as important I could be doing with my life than what I am doing now," she reports. I have spent a good amount of time in their home and have come to know them and the children well. This is my report on them.

In large measure, the Gordons have withdrawn from the mainstream of American society and culture. Ken and Elizabeth have concluded that they need to circle the wagons, as it were, in order to preserve and extend their racial and cultural heritage. While there is a television set in the home, I have never seen it on except a few times when the family watched a classic old film. I have not heard any popular music playing. I asked thirteen-year old Helen whether she ever wanted to watch television, take in one of the big movies showing in the theaters, or buy a pop music CD. I don't recall her exact words, but she said something to the effect that those activities are low and not worth her time.

"It is inconceivable to us," Ken told me, "that people actually sit in front of the television—videos included—hour upon hour, letting this degrading material into their homes. Something either inspires the soul or destroys it. For music, we listen to classical music. Our children read good books, play chess and backgammon, draw, paint, and sew. We take hikes as a family, go on picnics, cycle, and take in museums and concerts. We do things together in order to cement our bonds as a family."

There is also what the children *aren't* doing: they aren't attending to the persona and career of a pop musician; they aren't pressing their parents to come up with the cash for the latest video game; they aren't preoccupied with the plot twist of a television show; they aren't stewing over the fate of a professional sports team; and they aren't chattering on about a blockbuster film.

As far as I can tell, Ken and Elizabeth are successfully pulling off this embargo of the mass media. Before my contact with these parents, I would have said that whatever the merits of getting the mass media out of the lives of one's children, as a practical matter it is impossible. The mass media, along with computer technology, so I assumed, are so ubiquitous and enticing they are going to embed themselves in the lives of your children no matter what you do. Now I think that if parents are clear enough and committed enough, it is possible to keep Hollywood and music company moguls and television executives and website creators out of your children's lives.

I asked Elizabeth what she wants most for her children. "Honor," she immediately answered. "I want them to live an honorable life." Ken, who was sitting nearby, concurred. "Your honor means everything. Today, too few people understand that."

"There is an old concept of wanting more for your children than you yourself had," Elizabeth told me. "And part of that is you want them to have a better education than you did, or at least as good. With today's schools as they are, that isn't going to happen. Standards have been lowered. Kids aren't being pushed in school. When Ken and I were going through school, you would fail if you didn't do your work. But now everyone passes. There is a leveling going on in the schools. They operate so that no one is lower and no one is higher. The gifted children aren't really encouraged to excel. The students don't spend enough time reading now, and they aren't taught to think and analyze. Schools just seem to plod along day after day and little gets done. So many of the children don't want be there, and they just waste their own time and others' time."

"The worse kind of child abuse is to deny a child a decent education," Ken interjected. "One of the strengths of this country was our public school system, but not now. We've lost something terribly important. Today's graduates couldn't compete with the graduates at the turn of the last century. And I'll be frank with you: I think the integration of the schools and immigration patterns since the 1960s have had something to do with that. Our schools are reflecting the needs and styles of a new clientele, and people like us are paying the price for it. Look, you aren't going to understand what is going on in education if you don't take race into account—the direction Federal programs take, the problems with city schools, what content is stressed, testing, whatever you are talking about. The schools are providing what amounts to an education for a lesser people, not a great people. We point out more things to our children than the schools would. The schools are producing clones, everybody the same. A superior educational system promotes difference, not sameness. This whole egalitarian push that is the current fashion works against the advancement of the race. It is anti-selection. It keeps everybody at the level of the mediocre. Although then again maybe that is what those in charge of the society want—it makes us easier to control."

"The problem from a racial standpoint," Elizabeth offered, "is that we aren't, as we once were, with our own. I want my kids to be in a stable environment, not one where there are various factions. Kids need stability. We used to have pride in our race and our heritage. We were proud of our forefathers. Now, if a white child says he is proud of his lines, proud of his race, he is considered a racist. And that is not the case at all; there is nothing wrong for anyone to be proud of his race. There is nothing wrong with being proud of the civilization your people have created."

"Before, Washington and Jefferson were our heroes," Ken added. "Now, our idols are being wiped out and replaced by people like Martin Luther King. King was immoral and decadent and had communist ties, and he is being held up to our children as a hero. If you want to bring down a people, you rewrite their history and teach that to their children. You cut off children's roots so they have nothing to tie into. They have abolished the study of Latin in the schools. Knowledge of Latin is essential to an educated person, and it is part of this cutting us off from our racial and cultural roots. Over eighty percent of English words are derived from Latin. The Latin language has greatly influenced the development of the West. We make sure our children study Latin. There has been more than just a dumbing down in the schools. There has been a *twisting* down. The story of our race is being twisted. It is being perverted."

"James [their fifteen-year-old] is studying the Roman Empire now," Elizabeth pointed out. "That is opening up his imagination and it is connecting him to his heritage. He is reading great books about the Romans, classic books. Schools are getting rid of the old classics—fiction as well as non-fiction—and replacing them with, I guess, more acceptable writings, by non-entities."

I talked to James about what he is reading. He said he is reading about Alexander the Great, whom he really admires. "He made history. I want to do that." Among the things he has recently read, he told me, are *Quo Vadis*, *Thomas Jefferson and His World*, a book about John Paul Jones, some books about explorers of the world, the Hobbit series, *Alice in Wonderland*, *Arundel* by the historical novelist Kenneth Roberts, and some of the writings of Dostoevsky, Chekhov and Joseph C. Lincoln. He recommended that I read Roberts' book, *The Northwest Passage*, and gave me his copy to take with me when I went home. What I pick up from James is that he is on a quest: he is reaching out to learn; he is studying things. In contrast, so many youngsters his age go to class and do assignments and receive, in most cases, good grades, but they are not actually *studying* anything.

"I'm sure that some school professionals would say that you are brainwashing your children," I remarked to Ken.

"We teach them about their heritage," he responded, "the heritage of Western man. We give our children the best that our civilization has produced. The public schools aren't doing that. We don't get into every culture and subculture because we don't think those things are important in a primary sense. Is this brainwashing? It would really be ironic if the schools were to say we are brainwashing our children because that is exactly what *they* are doing. They are imposing doctrinaire opinions about the irrelevance of race in any positive or negative way. They are pushing a concept of the role of women in society that in our view is unnatural. And they are promoting internationalism. Schools are brainwashing white children to feel guilty about their heritage and turn away from it. Our children's heritage includes Homer, Plato, Michelangelo, Shakespeare, and Beethoven. They have every right to be overwhelmingly proud of their people. Absolutely, white children are being strictly brainwashed. Schools are molding them into the shape they want them to be in—raceless, historyless, malleable citizens of the world."

"I know you are Catholics. What about a Catholic school?"

"No," Ken answered. "We are seeing the same problems in private schools that we see in the public schools. And as for Catholic schools, the problem is even worse because the religious aura they have demands acquiescence from the children to what the school is putting out."

As time went along, I came to be aware that the two girls in this New Hampshire family, Helen and eleven-year-old Suzanna, always wore dresses. I asked Ken whether this was because my visits were viewed as dress-up occasions. No, he replied, most all of the time the girls wear dresses. It underscores what he and his wife believe to be the natural and healthy differences between boys and girls. "We teach our girls that being a good mother is the most important and accomplished thing they can possibly do with their lives. We believe that becoming a careerist, as is being pushed on girls by the feminists and the schools and the entertainment industry, is a dead end. For our boys, we promote all the manly virtues—responsibility, courage, hard work, and leadership."

The last time I visited the New Hampshire family I spent a good amount of time with Helen. Helen has the bearing of a fifteen-year old and I have had to keep reminding myself that she is only thirteen. She showed me some stories she had written along with the illustrations she had drawn to accompany them, and I read aloud from her stories. She told me of the impressive list of books she had read and was reading, and of her love for horses. Throughout our time together, Helen was steady-eyed, positive, considerate, confident, unthreatened, respectful, self-expressive, and interested in me.

At one point, I asked the question adults invariably ask: "I know it's a long way away, Helen, but have you thought about college and what you want to do when you are older?" It has been my experience that, these years, most girls—in good part, I think it fair to say, influenced by feminist ideology—aspire to college and a career, say, as a pilot or lawyer or business executive. But not Helen. She matter-of-factly and self-assuredly replied to my inquiry, "No, I don't want to go to college. I want to train and board horses. I want a family."

James intends to be a mathematician, he told me, and perhaps he will take over his father's actuarial business. As does Helen, James seems older, more mature, than other children his age. My contact with Helen and James, as well as other children in similar families, has prompted me to speculate about whether today's parents, schools, the media, and the peer culture keep children unduly childish. James strikes me as a proud and independent young man. He doesn't deck himself out in a costume and hairstyle or take on physical mannerisms that signal that he is in a separate tribe from the rest of us. I get no sense that he is trying to be a "babe magnet," as so many boys are, even in early adolescence. I mentioned to James that many people assume that since he hasn't been part of the school-based peer culture he lacks social skills. "That's ridiculous," he quickly and forcefully responded. "If you're congenial you can get along with anyone." I found myself trying to remember the last time I heard a teenager use the word congenial.

Ken and Elizabeth want their children to relate to others their age, but they are not hesitant about charting directions and imposing controls in this area. They believe children are like sponges: absorbent and easily shaped. They approve and disapprove of their children's activities and associations. They want to know, at every moment, where their children are and whom they are with and what they are doing. They make sure they meet the children their children associate with and their parents—in effect, they screen their children's contacts.

"I believe my children socialize much better than their peers do," Elizabeth asserts. "They can relate to people their own age and older people, too. My children socialize with whom they want about what they want, whether it be children their own age or adults. James has a couple of friends he is close to who share his ideas and interests. He says that there are a lot of children he simply has no interest in relating to. He has nothing in common with them. He is interested in history and math, and all they want to talk about are CDs and sports."

For the people like Ken and Elizabeth, physical activity tends to be things like boating and hiking and swimming, or perhaps tennis or golf—not soccer practice every night of the week. "The great outdoors—hiking and camping and climbing," says Ken. "But, with us, there is no emphasis on organized sports." Ken and Elizabeth believe that schools and commercial interests—sport exhibition companies like the Yankees and Lakers, the television networks, Nikes, and the rest—make something that is trivial and tangential in life seem vitally important and a core concern.

"So many other children James' age are starting to get caught up with dating and taking on a kind of gregarious personality in order to be accepted by the group," Elizabeth points out. "But why should he do that? Why do you have to connect with everybody?"

"You don't have to," Ken adds, "unless you want to be a life insurance salesman. We want our children to socialize, but where it is appropriate and safe. We have been there and we want to impart what we have learned to our children. We want them to be with other kids, but we want them to do it morally and honestly and with integrity and without losing their souls, which could easily happen. Life can be very unforgiving. Getting in with the wrong people can ruin someone's life forever. This is why we are so fervent about setting up protected environments and training our children from the beginning on correct socialization, correct interaction, and correct activities, so that when we are no longer here they will be able to be proud of themselves and carry on their heritage and their race."

Robert S. Griffin

16   MY OWN LITTLE CRUSADE

Rob Freeman is thirty-three and lives with his wife and daughter in Connecticut. He works in appliance repair. He has a intense, earnest persona.

For white kids of my generation, it seemed as if our heritage was taken away from us. We grew up with no place in the world, that's what it felt like. My parents and most of the parents of the kids I knew were liberals, and they didn't pass on a legacy of who we were. They didn't give us an identity. I don't know if you ever read the novel by the Dostoevsky, *The Possessed*. It is about an intergenerational problem between liberal parents and their children. That is what it was like for me and my friends. The '60's generation, our parents, didn't respect the traditional values of the generation before them, and the result was that their own children grew up in a vacuum. I respect my parents, I revere them, but I kind of had to raise myself. I had to find an identity and figure out what adulthood was on my own.

I became very conservative at a young age, when I was a teenager. I saw American as terminally corrupt. I'm a very passionate person and very concerned about things, that is just how I am. Other people my age didn't seem to care one way or another about anything important. They just wanted to have a good time and buy a car or something. They really didn't care about the future. They didn't care about the environment, or the changing racial demographics in the country, or the degradation of the food supply, or the ill health of Americans. Half of American citizens are overweight and something like thirty percent are obese, and that is a preventable problem. People don't know our history, and that is why we keep getting driven into one war after another. I saw America as being on a collision course with destruction. I'd tell that to people around me—well, I still do—and they'd laugh at me and scorn me.

The only people who have taken me seriously, and this was later on in my twenties, were the white nationalists. For a while, I hung out with environmentalists, Earth First was the organization, but they were a bunch of Marxists. I said to them, "The only thing an average citizen can do is practice local agriculture. That's where we can start. Let's start doing local agriculture." But they just wanted to protest and put down white people. They hated white people. I realized that the environmentalist movement, at least the people I was around, had been completely co-opted. It was just another branch of communism that was put in place to fake us out.

It got to the point that I wanted to opt out of this society. I decided I wanted to emigrate to Russia and stay there. I even learned the Russian language. This was when I was about nineteen. As it turned out, I went on to college instead, Connecticut College. I remember espousing conservative views in my classes and the Jewish kids shouting me down. At the time, I didn't make the connection between their being Jewish and their aggression toward me, but I got extremely angry that they were violating the rules of civility in a classroom. I wish I could turn back the clock and say to them, "You people should act like 'gentile-men.'" You know, a play on words: gentlemen, gentilemen? That would be perfect, because these Jewish kids were rude. They didn't belong in an intellectual environment where everybody's views are respected. By shouting me down, I see that now, these Jewish kids were censoring me.

There was a government class. This was in the fall of 1990, I think. I was majoring in Russian history and I had learned about the Bolsheviks and how they sent people to the gulags who didn't agree with them. A lot, if not most, of the Soviet regime at that time were Jewish, and they were the ones behind these things, like the extermination of seven or eight million Ukrainian farmers who didn't go along with their system. My Russian history teacher had tried to hide the connection between Jews and communism. She outright told us not to think about that. But I did think about that, and actually my Russian studies at Connecticut College pushed me towards becoming a white nationalist.

I would bring up some of the things I was learning from my Russian history class in my political science class, which was supposed to be an open exchange of ideas where we would enlighten one another, and the Jews would cut me off and start yelling. The guy teaching the class didn't do anything about it. He really wasn't in charge, and this was true in a lot of my classes—the adults weren't in charge. The kids were in charge. They had formed this left-wing Marxist tyranny. I realized that something terribly wrong was going on. Even if my views weren't perfect, we should've discussed them. That experience in that class planted a seed in me.

After college, I lived in Russia for six months. I tried to stay there, but I couldn't find a job, so I came back to this country. I spent time in the army reserves as a Russian linguist. I got a temporary duty assignment because I was one of the best Russian linguists in the army. During that time, I saw that the federal government was very corrupt. There were a lot of things, but the big thing that got me was they protected a couple of Jewish gangsters who stole millions of dollars from Russia. I was reading articles about the case in Russian newspapers—you couldn't read about it in our papers. I saw this one picture in the paper of an old man, and his face was screwed up in anger and he was holding his fist—the Russians, it's like when we give the middle finger, they make a fist and put their thumb between the middle finger and their first finger and they point their thumb at you. That's what this old man was doing who had lost all his money in this particular bank. I felt bad for him and I was very angry that our government sided with the people who stole the money from him. I was horrified. I had grown up a strong patriot and I had a crisis of faith in the whole U.S. government. For the first time, I saw a Jewish connection with the problems I was seeing and I took note of that.

When my tour of duty ended with customs, I didn't ask for another one. This was in 1997. That is also the year that I met my wife, Anya, who is Ukrainian. We have a daughter who is going on five. The INS—the Immigration and Naturalization Service—gave Anya a hard time. They did all they could to deport her. They said she got married while on a student visa and that indicated that she had never intended to return to Ukraine when she came here to go to school. They discounted the possibility that she had intended to return but had met someone here and that had changed her plans. We tried to bring Anya's mother to this country to visit us and to see her grandchild, but the INS turned us down three times. They said that since she is a widow and doesn't own property she will likely try to stay, and that would put a burden on the social welfare system. At the same time they were doing that to us, Mexicans and El Salvadorians and Guatemalans and Africans were streaming in by the thousands every month. Even if they come in illegally, the government just kind of winks and looks the other way. And certainly any Jew can come to this country who wants to. I saw that when I was working at the INS. I was just getting more and more disgusted. I'm the sort of person who wants to look a little deeper and understand better what's going on, and that's what I've been trying to do.

Do you know about the Nushawn Williams case? He is a black rap artist from Brooklyn who went to the small town of Jamestown in upstate New York and infected at least nine girls with the AIDS virus. I read about it in *Harper's* magazine. The article made excuses for what this guy did and avoided obvious issues, like what has happened to their upbringing that nine young white girls—and I'll bet it was a lot more than that—give their bodies to this black guy? Where is their racial identity, their racial integrity? Race aside, where is their dignity as young women? You know what I mean? What is happening to our women? There was a time when blacks didn't dare mess with our women. Now they are in Jamestown, New York going through teenagers, and these girls were giving themselves to him and evidently nobody in the community cared that it was happening until they all became infected with HIV. What is going on? Is this the result of what these girls see on MTV and the movies Hollywood is putting out, or what? And where were their parents? What is happening to us? Who is doing this? What is going on?

I still don't know everything that is going on, but I am starting to figure things out. I remember when I was at Connecticut College and they had [Holocaust survivor] Eli Wiesel speak and I knew what he was saying couldn't be that way, that he was slanting things. But I didn't have the information I do now and so I couldn't stand up and ask a question that would break through all his lies. But I have more information now and I can stand up for myself better now, so I've decided to go on my own little crusade. I am going to get the Jews and liberals, smash through their deceptions. I am going public and speaking the truth, and it has been great, fantastic.

It started with the Framingham [Massachusetts] Human Relations Commission sessions in early 2002. I was living there—I just moved to Connecticut a couple of months ago. They had meetings once a month. They were like what went on in the old Soviet Union, sort of brainwashing sessions to educate the people on the proper way to think about race in this case. These kinds of indoctrinations depend on the absence of any dissent. I am a member of the National Alliance and I brought some other Alliance people with me and we would stand up and speak out against what they were doing. Even when we didn't talk we got to them. We would all sit in the front row and stare at them, and we could see how uncomfortable that made them. I was very glad of that. It seemed like I was doing my patriotic duty.

The first one we went to was on hate crimes. The town's attorney was there, and a few other "big-wigs" from the town. They started telling us how whites were committing all these hate crimes against minorities. I got a chance to speak and I said that European Americans were always getting depicted as the perpetrators of hate crimes and non-whites and homosexuals as the victims of hate crimes. I talked about how hate crimes are not enforced evenly and that they are reported unfairly. I said that we had all heard about Mathew Shepard and James Byrd, but very few people know about Kristopher Kime and Jason Befort and Heather Muller and Jesse Dirkhising. [As described earlier, in Jasper County, Texas in 1998, three white men beat and cut the throat of James Byrd, a black man, before chaining him by his ankles to a pick-up truck and dragging him to his death, decapitating him in the process. In Wyoming in 1998, Mathew Shepard, 21, a homosexual, died five days after being robbed and beaten mercilessly by two heterosexual men and left tied to a fence. Kristopher Kime, 20, white, was killed in 2001 during a rampage of blacks, who attacked whites during a Mardi Gras demonstration in Seattle, Washington, injuring seventy. Kime was killed by a black man who punched him and drove his head into the pavement when he came to the aid of a white woman who was being attacked. Jason Befort and Heather Muller were two of four white friends in their twenties who were shot and killed execution-style in 2000 in Wichita, Kansas as they knelt on the ground after being tortured and sexually assaulted for hours by two black men. A fifth white person, a woman, survived the gunshot and walked naked for a mile before finding help. Jesse Dirkhising was a thirteen-year-old Arkansas boy who, in 1998, was tortured, raped, and murdered by two homosexual men.] I got in the newspaper for that. They made fun of me. Basically they said I was angry and pathetic.

At the second human relations meeting the next month, there was a Jewish state senator woman, Deborah Bloomer, and she was going to lecture us on the Holocaust. With all the publicity we got the first time, the Framingham police were there, including the Chief of Police. Actually, he was kind of a good guy. He told me he didn't agree with us, but he respected our right of free speech. Well, I got up and said that the Holocaust story was full of holes and they won't let anybody really look into what happened, and that the whole Holocaust myth is a way to paint the Jews as victims and make gentiles feel guilty and defer to whatever Jews want.

You can imagine how that went over. I thought one guy was going to attack me in the meeting. When I got out into the street, the Anti-Racist Action—the ARA—had shown up. They are a group of communist Jews, and they had masks on and they were threatening violence. It was like gang warfare, us and the ARA. The police were very alarmed because they had never dealt with such a thing. As it turned out, there wasn't any violence, but some ARAs took pictures of us and put them on a web site—I guess to scare us.

Another one I'll tell you about is the baseball bat incident. This was this year up in Hamilton, Massachusetts. Hamilton is a peaceful little white town in the northern part of the state. The Jewish organization the Anti-Defamation League was doing these, like, kosher certification programs around the state. With the guidance of the Anti-Defamation League, towns would sort of make an official proclamation that they aren't a place that hates and they welcome non-whites into the town. A number of towns agreed to go through the program, but when the Anti-Defamation League approached Hamilton, the selectmen of the town said, no, we don't want to do it. We don't want to be in the business of supporting a private organization. So there was this big scandal. A little girl got on *Good Morning America* saying, "Oh, Hamilton is a place for hate!"

I read about all this in the newspaper and I thought, "Oh boy, this opens up a chance to oppose the Anti-Defamation League." So I set up a protest on Easter Sunday in Hamilton. We had signs that said, "Let's make Israel no place for hate" and "Stop the Jewish holocaust against the Palestinians" and "ADL, practice what you preach." If you recall, that same day there was an Israeli raid that killed Palestinians like crazy and it was very bad, so the timing turned out to be perfect. The Hamilton police were very nice to us, and people stopped and took packets of information from us. There were some hostile people, but for the most part people seemed pretty sympathetic.

As we were packing up and about to leave, a blue SUV pulls up and this gentleman who was very hostile got out. He was obviously Jewish and he was all mad and yelling. He said that it says in the Bible that that land in the Middle East belongs to the Jews and things like that. Eventually, his teenage son jumps out of the car with a baseball bat and starts swinging at me and the other people. The police chief of Hamilton was on his day off and in civilian clothes and he pulled up in his car just as the kid was swinging the bat at us. He got out of his unmarked vehicle and he said, "Son, give me the bat. I'm the Hamilton Police Chief," but the kid wouldn't give him the bat. The kid and the police chief struggled over the bat, and finally the chief got the bat away from the kid. He had called for backup and four police cruisers showed up and they arrested the kid and took statements from all of us, but they never did prosecute the case.

Shortly after the Hamilton incident, there was a feature article about me in the Boston Globe with a picture of me. My daughter was going to a Waldorf school. A lot of wealthy liberal people send their kids to Waldorf, many of them Jews. These people push diversity on everybody else, how great it is to go to school with blacks and all that, but they don't want that for their own kids, so they get them into these private schools. In the article about me, I didn't mention the school by name, but I did talk about the hypocrisy I was seeing. I said I had talked with one woman who has a child at the school about what she thought of the situation in Zimbabwe in Africa where the white farmers are getting murdered by blacks. I told her about how these mobs of blacks raid white farms and gang rape the women and torture and murder people and set buildings on fire. She said that she took the side of the blacks, that they were doing the right thing. I kind of ripped into her in the article.

The Waldorf administrators had a meeting with myself and my wife and they said, "The parents of the students here are really mad at you, and if they are mean to you or your daughter, don't retaliate, don't do anything back, just let this all run its course. You are just going to have to take whatever these parents dish out." I wanted my daughter to be able to stay in the school, so I said, "OK, fine," but my wife didn't want to put up with that. She said, "We're going to pull our daughter out of that school." My wife wasn't going to let our daughter to be subject to Jewish hate, the stares and the pointing and whispering. So we withdrew our daughter from the school.

We've just moved to Connecticut and there's a coffee shop we would go to now and then. Last week I went with my daughter for a cookie, and just after we got in the door, one of the women who owns the place came up to us and said, "I have read about you, and I don't want you in here." I said, "OK," and we left. If this woman had had any class she would have whispered it to me, but as it was she did it right in front of my daughter. My daughter was traumatized by the incident.

The most recent episode was up in Lewiston, Maine. Some refugee commission settled thousands of black Bantus from Somalia into Atlanta, Georgia. The Bantus didn't like it in Atlanta and they went looking for an area with good welfare benefits they could move to. They found their place in the little town of Lewiston, Maine, and about twelve hundred or so of them moved up there. The people in Lewiston started complaining to the mayor, saying, "What are all these people doing here?" So the mayor, Larry Raymond, responded with a public letter saying to the Bantus, "Slow down your influx, we're financially exhausted from it"—meaning the welfare costs and the need for special programs in the schools and everything. He didn't get into what it was doing to the white European culture of Lewiston to have all these Africans suddenly descend on them, which

I wish he would have done, but I guess that would have been too much to expect of any white elected official.

When the liberal media heard about what was going on in Lewiston, of course they praised all these blacks pouring in there to the skies and trashed anybody who had any objection to it as a racist. Mayor Raymond was supposed to have said, "We love diversity. Send us as many Bantus as you can get to come up here." He didn't do that and he had to pay for it. The media said he was a racist and called on him to resign. He responded in the way all whites these days do to the charge that they harbor improper racial thoughts. He knelt before the commissars and pleaded his innocence. He said that he wasn't a racist, really he wasn't; oh, please don't think that. He said that one of his sons or daughters, I don't remember which, had adopted two black kids, so he had two black grandchildren, and so, really, he wasn't a transgressor. He begged for mercy, but they didn't give it to him. Maybe if he had been a little more contrite they would have, but he didn't quite prostrate himself enough. They are still attacking him for the letter.

We figured we would give this Lewiston situation some energy. One of our people actually made contact with the Bantu elders and suggested that they go live in Miami with all the Jews. We told them that Miami had great welfare benefits and that Jews welcome diversity and would love for them to come and live with them. I gave a speech up in Lewiston and said that white people have a right to protect their way of life and to live among their own people. I said that self-preservation—cultural and racial survival—is the right of all people, that it needs no justification, that it is its own justification. I also talked about the assaults against whites going on and the rape of a white girl that had just happened.

I got some press coverage for the Lewiston speech and my wife is starting to get worried—you know, what will happen with her job or to our daughter or to me, and I understand that. I'm thinking of becoming an organic farmer out in the woods somewhere so we can just leave all this. I don't fit here. We don't fit here. Just our own little farm somewhere where my family can live, and I can grow enough food for us and, I hope, some of my white nationalist comrades. We will have to go a long way away to do that, though, because here in Connecticut they are bulldozing the farmland and building condominiums and "McMansions." My wife is looking into finding us some land to rent or buy and I'm supporting her in that. I like my job in appliance repair a lot, but I'm ready to be a farmer, I really am. I can't wait to set up my organic garden. Yeah, I'm going to quit all this activism stuff. Although, I see that there is a diversity symposium at my alma mater, Connecticut College, coming up. I think I might attend that.

Robert S. Griffin

17   TOWARD A LEGION EUROPA

Mike Rienzi* is in his late thirties and lives in the northeastern part of the United States and works as a researcher in the field of science. He is married and has a young child.

I grew up in the northeastern United States in an urban area. The ethnic composition of the neighborhood where my family lived had changed—before, it had been practically all white—but we didn't have enough money to move, so we were stuck there. The area had become predominantly non-white: African Americans, West Indians, Jamaicans, and, as time went on, Hispanics—Puerto Ricans, Dominicans, and Mexicans. My parents were politically right of center—Republican, conservative. They weren't what I would call racialists, but they were aware of the impact of race on what we were going through after the neighborhood changed. I don't think it is too much of a stretch to say that with the exception of Australian aboriginals, I experienced the gamut of human diversity growing up. I saw up close the reality of racial differences in intelligence and behavior and how that reality contrasts with the egalitarian rhetoric we're bombarded with constantly. I experienced the resentment and hate these other groups have toward whites. I experienced verbal harassment, and I was mugged and beaten. I saw, first hand, the unfairness—the absurdity, the insanity—of the various governmental policies that beat back white Americans. They use words like "affirmative action" and "equality" to justify these policies, but they are just clever euphemisms for outright racial discrimination.

People who think of themselves as enlightened and on the moral high ground in matters of race write off people like me as ignorant racists. Unlike them, so it goes, we pre-judge people. If only we were exposed to racial and ethnic diversity we would learn to value different kinds of people—etcetera, etcetera, you've heard the line. You'll notice that most of these people doing the pontificating and

154

finger pointing about racial equality and harmony and the virtues of integration and multi-racialism do it from the far distance of the leafy suburbs or a university campus somewhere. The fact of the matter is that, unlike practically all of them, I have lived close up with the reality of race in America. And regardless of what they might like to think, I am not stupid or unenlightened or their moral inferior. The people who look down their noses at people like me should come live for a year or two or three where my family and millions of other white families live. Let their children grow up and go to school in this pigsty and be threatened and attacked and robbed and raped. Then they can talk.

I had a number of close Jewish friends growing up and spent a lot of time in their homes. It was then that I got my first exposure to the contrast between Jews' liberalism when it comes to the United States and their conservatism and hawkishness when it comes to Israel. I got an initial sense of the difference between the face Jews show the world and what they are like in private. I remember one time I was invited to a Bar Mitzvah where the rabbi got pretty vocal. I guess he didn't know there were any gentiles there. Anyway, he went on denouncing gentiles and Christianity and saying that Jews were the chosen people and so on. I was really young then, but that was an eye-opening experience for me. As I went higher in education and got more involved in science, I continued to have a lot of contact with Jews. So my views on Jews aren't just based on what I have read or heard.

My political outlook started to get shaped in the 1980s. I was living in the city and Reagan came along with his talk about welfare queens and being against affirmative action and so forth, and that connected with me. I thought—foolishly, I now realize—that Reagan and the Republicans might actually do something about the situation I was in. I was happy that Reagan was elected the first time and then re-elected, and I became immersed in conservative Republican politics. Eventually, though, I became disenchanted with that whole scene. It finally became clear to me that Reagan and the other conservative Republicans weren't going to do anything for white Americans. There were some foreign policy achievements around the Cold War, but during the Reagan years illegal immigrants got amnesty, there were all sorts of racial preferences and double standards, and the whole political correctness movement really got going.

When Bush came along in '88 and started talking about Willy Horton in the campaign, I saw the Republican pattern of moving slightly to the right to get white votes and then forgetting about whites once they got elected. [To make the point that his opponent, Michael Dukakis, was soft on crime, a Bush campaign ad—some thought it had racial overtones—pointed out that when Dukakis was governor of Massachusetts, a furlough was granted to convicted murderer, Willie Horton, an African American. Horton used his furlough to punch, pistol-whip, kick, and cut a white man, Clifford Barnes. When Barnes' fiancée returned that evening, Horton gagged her and savagely raped her.] Of course, now they don't even bother pandering to whites. Bush junior is so concerned about attracting minority votes, Hispanics in particular, he stays clear of saying anything that might sound like it has the interest of white Americans in mind.

As time went on, I came to see that arguments over tax cuts and those kinds of things are picayune compared to the racial issues we face in this country. I've come to think of the Republicans as an opiate, a safety valve—they give whites the false sense that if they are disenchanted with the way things are going, voting for Republicans is going to make things better. You had the '96 election with Bob Dole and Jack Kemp. Dole pitched himself as a "civil rights Republican" and told the delegates at the convention something to the effect that anyone who didn't have an "inclusive" attitude could leave the convention hall. And Kemp is a well-known panderer to blacks, Hispanics, and Jews. And there was Colin Powell going on about the virtues of affirmative action. Really, it would be good if the Republicans went so overboard sucking up to minorities that it would finally sink in to whites that the two party system is a myth. What we have now is one liberal party with two marginally different wings, neither of which gives a damn about the future of whites as a race.

In the early '90s, I read Jared Taylor's book, *Paved with Good Intentions*. It laid out the reality of the racial situation in this country and put things into perspective for me. I started to subscribe to

Taylor's newsletter, *American Renaissance*. *AR* really brings home the seriousness of the problems blacks and Hispanics represent to whites in this country. I'm talking about things like black-on-white crime—the assaults and robberies and murders and rapes—and the destruction of our schools and cities and the debasement of our culture. Debates over the capital gains tax miss the point of what is happening in America that is truly significant. *AR* also brings home the reality that the problems whites face—which are really problems of basic survival—are global and not just limited to this country.

In the mid-'90s, I became a regular listener to William Pierce and Kevin Strom's *American Dissident Voices* short-wave radio broadcasts. Those programs not only dealt with the racial issues per se, they also got into the whole Jewish issue, that so many things going on that bring down white people are promoted by Jews either individually or through their organizations. Even before listening to the *ADV* broadcasts I had a basic idea of the negative influence of Jews on white interests, but Strom and Pierce gave specific examples and they got it across in forceful and clear language.

I work in the science field and have a scientific mentality, I guess you could say. I try to look at things objectively and weigh the evidence and test which of the competing hypotheses is valid. I compared what the establishment was saying about the issues of race and immigration and the future of this country and so on with what William Pierce was saying. I asked myself, which of them squares best with my experience? The answer: Pierce does. *American Renaissance* would report a story that it said the mainstream press had suppressed. I'd look into it and, indeed, the story was true, and it was important, and the mainstream press had kept it from public attention, from white attention.

The magazines and broadcasts would mention books and Internet links, and I would check them out. I read academic books on genetics and heredity by Rushton and Lynn and others [J. Phillippe Rushton and Richard Lynn], and mainstream books about history and current affairs. I read in detail all three of Kevin MacDonald's books [*A People That Shall Dwell Alone*; *Separation and Its Discontents*; and *The Culture of Critique*]. The pieces were starting to fit together for me. I reached the conclusion that peoples of European descent can be thought of as either a single bio-cultural group or a conglomeration of closely related bio-cultural groups. I also concluded that Jews have genetic and cultural and political interests which sharply deviate from those of European Americans, and they vigorously and effectively pursue those interests to the detriment of white people. I reached the point where I could say with certainty that what the racial nationalists are saying about the problems that exist is right and what the establishment is saying is wrong. We need a radical restructuring of society based on racial nationalist principles. White Americans need separatism. We need our own culture, our own schools, our own media, our own communities, our own leaders, our own way of life.

Whites are being slowly decimated. Our connection to one another, our connection to our own heritage, our way of life, our numbers, all of it is being slowly but surely eroded. Most Americans are so brainwashed by the media and the schools and so caught up with ballgames and other nonsense that they never wake up to that reality. We've become so hyper-individualistic that when we see the problem we are likely to say, "Well, I'm only going to care about myself and protect myself." Hyper-individualism is one of the major flaws we have now as a people.

The question for me is what my personal response is going to be to the situation I see. I know I could say, "I'm going to die, so why should I care what the racial composition of America is in 2050 or 2100?" But I do care. I feel connected to European peoples. That is where my genetic and ethnic and cultural roots are. That's where my interests are. It is sort of like what Pierce said in that biography you wrote about him [*The Fame of a Dead Man's Deeds*]: if you really connect with yourself, you discover that you feel a responsibility to your people who came before you and those that will follow you, and you want your culture and your race to survive after you are gone. If your race does survive, that will give you a kind of immortality: what you are genetically and culturally will continue; in a way, *you* will continue. The idea that in a hundred or two hundred or three hundred years my race and what we have done and what we represent won't exist is just not unacceptable to me. I will do what I can to help us get on a better path as a race than we are on now.

I see a real necessity for peoples of European descent—whether you call them whites or European Americans or Euros, whatever term you want to use—to start developing a more collective and cohesive mindset. We need to start moving toward identity politics like the other groups are already doing. We have to start thinking of ourselves as European Americans with particular interests, and we need to start establishing structures and organizations to pursue those interests. The point I have been making is that I don't think the Republican Party is likely to be a vehicle for serving a white agenda. Of course anything is possible, but I think the neoconservatives, most all of them Jews, are so entrenched in the Republican party that it would be better to start a third party.

I have no illusion that anytime soon you are going to see a racially aware white candidate run for president. But you could start to have racialist candidates for local offices. They aren't going to win, but they could get the message out, encourage some thought and dialogue. People could be recruited for the campaign and then network and stay in contact, maybe to engage in community activism and mutual support. Some people might say that third party candidates would draw votes away from the Republicans. But it should be clear that I see the Republican Party as a millstone around the neck of white people. The status quo is very bad for white people, and that is what the Republican Party represents. Since 9/11 especially, they have been distracting us with phony-baloney patriotism and telling us to keep consuming and watching the war on TV while our people march off a cliff racially.

It seems to me that every other racial group in America except whites has organizations at a local, community level that look out for their interests. Whites are completely atomized. Let me give you an example from an article I just read. It is about a Jewish community in New York State. This community is completely segregated and separatist. If the government would try to break up that neighborhood with so-called fair housing laws and low income housing and bring in minorities to integrate the schools there, these Jews are organized well enough to damn well put a stop to it. No one dares break up these Jewish areas. And consider the example of Asians. They help each other out financially, so they aren't dependent on banks. They give each other loans and they help each other get started in business. Asians aren't so individualistic. Whites have to learn to be that way more. They are going to have to start thinking of themselves in collective terms the way these other groups do and not just as individuals or families.

Frankly, I'm not encouraged by most of what I see in the white racial movement currently. There are too many nitwits and hyper-extremists and dysfunctional types waiting around for some sort of revolution while they talk and do nothing, or a few of them blow something up or shoot somebody, which just reinforces the negative stereotype white racialists have with the mass of people. I think the challenge is to heighten whites' racial awareness—especially the sane, honest, hardworking, law-abiding whites—and convince them to form voluntary, private organizations in their own communities. These organizations would exist to do practical things. The problem now is you have racialist organizations and they say, "Join up and send us your membership dues," and you get a little membership card and a newsletter once a month. But the members stay isolated and everything stays divorced from reality. We need racial nationalist organizations that help children with homework, and help old and infirmed people, and that clean up neighborhoods, and where everybody stands together when some outside force tries to push them around. Maybe these organizations could have youth auxiliaries.

As it is now, we have white people thinking, "What am I going to do? I have got to send my children to the local school and it's full of minorities and they are going to be taught all sorts of nonsense and they are going to get attacked, and my neighborhood is deteriorating, and my life is going to hell." An activist comes up to them and says, "Let's go protest against the United States' foreign policy in the Middle East." That's great, our foreign policy in the Middle East should be protested, but there is still the question of what is going to be done to help the person scratching his head trying to figure out what he is going to do about what is happening in his life. At a very basic level we have to protect ourselves physically.

The Nation of Islam may be an example of the kind of thing I'm talking about. It was founded in the 1930s, but it wasn't until the early 1960s that most white Americans ever heard about the Black

Muslims. They spent decades building a base of support in the black community by helping black people with whatever they were doing in their community. So when they started becoming vocal and white people in the early 1960s started saying, "Hey, these people are a problem, what are we going to do?" it was already too late. The Black Muslims were already firmly established and had become an integral part of black society. In a similar way, a white nationalist movement has to grow like a plant, with its roots firmly in the soil.

What I am talking about is separatism. We need to ask ourselves how the Jews in that article I told you about can get away with being separatists and we can't. It's because they have a group identity and they are organized at the local level. Saying this, I don't mean to imply that I think all the action should be at the local level. We need to carry on the fight on many fronts—at the level of ideas, in the arts, at the national and international levels, the full spectrum. I'm just underscoring that we need to create structures that will help us network and take action right where we are at the grassroots level.

I've become interested in the ideas of a Romanian activist and intellectual by the name of Comeliu Condreanu. Condreanu formed the Legion of Archangel Michael in Romania back in the 1920s. He emphasized what I have been talking about here: that before you have large-scale power, you can get things done through activism at the local level. Condreanu promoted the idea of a "new man," which in his case meant a new and better type of Romanian. So his was a spiritual and moral movement as much as it was a cultural and political one. Along the lines of Condreanu's thinking, I am interested in the idea of the creation of white legionnaires—a Legion Europa, if you will. The Legion Europa would be a perspective, a way of looking at things. It would be an informal association or network. It would be a collection of local organizations that would bring together all European peoples, all white people, and be concerned about actions and results and the enhancement of personal qualities of its members.

A measure of any organization, whether it is of the Legion Europa sort I've been talking about or some other, is what kind of people it attracts and what influence it and its leaders have on those who become a part of it. A good organization moves its members in the direction of greater racial and cultural identity and pride, and toward greater responsibility for themselves and to other European people and their future. It supports them moving in the direction of a more honorable way of looking at things and a more honorable, upstanding way of living their lives.

www.ingramcontent.com/pod-product-compliance
Lightning Source LLC
Chambersburg PA
CBHW022232290526
45785CB00014B/742